Value-Centered Leadership

A Survivor's Strategyfor Personal and Professional Growth

George A. Burk

Heuristic Books
Chesterfield MO 63006-7151

Graphics Credits:
The cover photograph of Captain Burk by Jon P. Jones.
ISBN 1-888725-59-1
First Printing, January, 2004
Heuristic Books

Library of Congress Cataloging-in-Publication Data

Burk, George A., 1941-
  Value-centered leadership : a survivor's strategy for personal and professional growth / George A. Burk.
    p. cm.
  ISBN 1-888725-59-1 (regular print, Heuristic Books : alk. paper) -- ISBN 1-888725-54-0 (large print (16pt) Macro-PrintBooks : alk. paper)
  1. Leadership. 2. Values. 3. Leadership--Moral and ethical aspects. I. Title.
  HD57.7.B86 2004
  658.4'092--dc22

                              2004006239

PO Box 7151
Chesterfield, MO 63006-7151
(636) 394-4950
heuristicbooks.com

Who is George Burk?

In 1998, Captain George Burk's USAF (Ret.) story of his experience as a plane crash and burn survivor, *The Bridge Never Crossed–A Survivor's Search for Meaning,* generated an outburst of praise from everyone who read it. On May 4, 1970, George was the sole survivor of 14 Air Force personnel in a military plane crash. He suffered extensive burns, and multiple internal injuries. This motivational speaker and author returns with another book presenting many of the lessons and principles of life learned as a survivor and "overcomer."

George Burk is a highly decorated military officer and public servant who presently resides in Scottsdale, Arizona. He is a nationally recognized motivational speaker, trainer and writer whose mission is to "entertain, inform, inspire and persuade."

As a plane crash and burn survivor, George Burk shares with you his experiences, principles, and values you can use on your journey; they are valid and work because George uses them in his own life.

Whether you are a professional immersed in a search for organizational change, excellence, and quality improvement, or an individual looking for ways to improve your personal life, you will find invaluable information in *Value-centered Leadership — A Survivor's Strategy for Personal and Professional Growth.*

In a refreshingly straightforward and sometimes humorous style, George Burk shares his unique insights and perspectives into effective leadership, meaningful change, core values, and what it takes to be an effective leader. He offers the suggestion, based on his unique experiences, that for any change to be effective, it must be sequential, that is inside out — not outside in.

George writes that life is filled with joy and adversity. It is adversity which is part of life's test, which makes us stronger. These adversities include obstacles, challenges and sufferings. He shares with you the idea that failure is not falling down, but staying down. In *Value-Centered Leadership*, the reader will learn the importance of a positive attitude, and how honesty, integrity and the deeply imbedded desire to live play in a person's journey through life.

George takes the example of Jesus and how He took a disorganized staff of twelve "employees" and built them into an organization that still exists 2,000 years later. The principles Jesus used to secure the apostle's commitment and enrollment is still valid today. George has also included "Chapter Checkpoints," which are thoughtful questions that help focus your thinking, plan your approach, and challenge you to "benchmark" some issues you may have forgotten. The chapter's checkpoints can also help enhance team effectiveness and team productivity with dynamic outcomes.

Perhaps there are people in your life you have not thanked in awhile, patted on the back, or with whom you have lost touch. *Value-Centered Leadership* seeks to remind you of what is truly important and challenges you to appreciate what and who you have.

Value-Centered Leadership is a simple, profound, and fresh approach to effectively lead others to be self-motivated. This book will provide ways to establish core values while leading yourself and others.

Captain George Burk
P.O. Box 6392
Scottsdale AZ 85261-6392
1-800-769-8568
website:http://www.georgeburk.com
    email:gburk@georgeburk.com

To Olga
My Poulaki
"Sagapo"

Value-Centered Leadership

A Survivor's Strategy for Personal and Professional Growth

George A. Burk

ACKNOWLEDGEMENTS

"Without innovation there is no knowledge."
—Albert Einstein

"And without knowledge, there is no innovation"
—George Burk

I thank my wife, Olga, for her unwavering support and encouragement for this and my other undertakings.

I thank Jerry Melarangio, Mike Kazyak, Jim McGregor, Ron Reeves, Mike Crowe, Joe Gorriaz, Dr. Stanley Caine, and Reverend Ken Semon. These individuals have read several drafts of the manuscript and have offered their invaluable insights and experiences on how to make it more meaningful.

I thank Ruth Merillat, Helen Johnson, Deborah Weisberg, Tom Morrissey, Jeff DeBell, Larry Smith, Kevin Sell, Walter Buerkle, Nancy Bohn, Marilyn Lambeth and Fred LaFamina for their thoughts about the book's content, organization, and focus. Jim Hartley, John Arms and Deborah Adams for their incisive feedback which helped shape important ideas and asked, "Why is George writing this?"

I was amazed and encouraged by the willingness of these individuals to offer their suggestions and feedback openly and to relate to me their successes and challenges about personal and professional experiences.

I thank my family and friends and countless others who have helped make my journey rewarding, challenging and exciting.

Thanks to all of you for your love, friendship, support, and guidance.

> **"True friendships are not measured in the multitudes, but in their worth and choice."**
> **—George Burk**

Value-Centered Leadership

A Survivor's Strategy for
Personal and Professional Growth

Table of Contents

PREFACE

"Self-pity is our worst enemy, and if we yield to it,
we can never do anything wise in the world."
—Helen Keller

On a foggy, rainy day in May, 1970, I was part of a fourteen member Air Force crew that took-off on an inspection mission. A few minutes after take-off, I opened my eyes and discovered I was lying outside a burning plane in a pasture in the rolling hills of Northern California.

I was burned, cold and scared, and I felt that my life had zipped past me like a freight train. I had never felt so alone and helpless; I sensed that my survival was a long-shot at best. At that moment, while I lay there, and for several months thereafter, my instinct told me that if I had any chance to live, I had to reach inside myself to a place that I didn't know existed. I had to mentally call upon the values my parents and others had taught me in order to survive this ugly and unimaginable ordeal.

I pleaded with God to give me a second chance to live.

The 89 days I spent in the Intensive Care Unit (ICU) and the 18 months in the hospital were long and arduous. I remained fairly lucid during the first ten days in the ICU and was aware of the nurses and doctors around my bed. In fact, when I heard voices, I opened my eyes and always saw my doctor, nurses and corpsmen work on me. They desperately tried to make me as comfortable as possible. Nothing in my life could have ever prepared me for my pain and discomfort. The pain from the burns seemed to reach deep into my soul and traumatize me unlike any other type of injury or illness before in my life. In fact, if all the illnesses and injuries I experienced prior to the plane crash

1

were combined, they would not even come close to the pain I endured in the ICU.

It was during these moments that I disciplined myself to use the positive energies in my life in order to try and block out as much of the physical pain as possible. I often thought about my family and how I wanted to live and not die in that place at that time. It was this mind-set and focus that also helped me to deal with the many obstacles I had to endure.

I knew there would be times when the pain was so intense that it would tempt me to give up and die. But in my mind, I knew what I needed to do and the proper course of action I needed to take. If I had any chance to live and not die, I would have to reach into the deepest recesses of my mind and soul and find the reason to live. I had a lot of "whys" in my life – my wife, children, family and friends -- and it was up to me to find the "how's" – how I would find the mental and physical strength to persevere.

My parents, especially my mother, always encouraged me when she said, "Always do your best and never give up and know that I will always love you." My mother was not talking about perfection, but striving for excellence.

The strategy of having my actions mirror my words also became an integral part of this philosophy. I believe all of us have guardian angels who watch over us and who protect us from harm. Our angels are that inner voice we often hear tell us, "Do not say that," or, "Do not go there," or "Something about this place or person does not seem quite right." When my subconscious mind, or when my angel tells me that I am doing something that is proper and correct, that is the voice to which I try to listen.

For a number of years after the crash, I experienced what contemporary mental health professionals call, "Survivor Guilt" and "Post-Traumatic Stress Disorder (PTSD)." At the time, I did not know about these psychological terms and did not take a lot of time or energy to think about them. I was too busy trying to recapture my life and starting to act like a survivor and not a victim. A vital part of my personal "survivorship" has always been holding myself responsible and accountable for my choices. There were times when I wondered why I had been singled out to experience something as painful and gruesome as the severe burns and the numerous internal injuries I sustained in the plane crash. However, I would be shaken back to reality when I recalled how my parents struggled through an economic depression and a world war. They did whatever it took to feed and clothe their family, buy a home, pay their bills, and educate their children. I remember my parents when they used paper to conceal the holes in the soles of their shoes because they lacked the money to have their shoes repaired. These thoughts helped me understand that I was not the only person who had ever experienced hardship.

My parents had little formal education. My father had to drop out of school after the eighth grade to work and help support his family. My parents, and many individuals I knew when I was young, lived the leadership and quality improvement principles written about today in books, magazines, and newspapers.

Those principles and values included: Faith, Accountability, Responsibility, Trust, Integrity, Teamwork, Duty, Honor, and Patriotism. The economic circumstances of those times required they walk the talk!

My parents, relatives, and others like them had neither the time, inclination, nor the luxury to feel sorry for themselves because they were too busy trying to make a living. Feeling sorry for themselves, seeking pity, or expecting someone else to solve their problems was not the way they lived. They empowered themselves out of economic necessity, hunger, and the need to survive.

My parents and my extended family were my internal anchors. My mother had a backbone like a steel rod when it came to believing in me.

Our country is filled with stories of how people overcame hardships and survived. They used their personal adversity to spur them to bigger and better things in life for themselves and their families.

Although I have never met him, I heard a similar story of a young boy who left the hardships and economic deprivation of his native Greece in 1914 and came to this country to pursue his dream of living in America. On the day he left his family and friends, George Koutsogiannakis was a 16 year-old who ran as fast as he could through the olive groves near his village of Hora in Peloponese in the hills of southern Greece. While his mother cried and pleaded for him to come back, he yelled over his shoulder that he had to go to America.

George was determined to pursue his dreams.

Many times as a young boy, he would lie on the ground in the stand of olive trees, gaze at the stars and wonder if the people in America saw the same stars. On the day he left, unable to speak English and walking with a club foot, he climbed onto a ship with hundreds of other immigrants. With his $200 life savings in his worn and frayed pants, he started a journey which would fulfill his dreams.

Imagine the courage, strength, and faith this young boy possessed that made him want to leave his parents and friends and travel to a strange land thousands of miles away. George passed through Ellis Island in 1914. He taught himself English, Spanish, and how to play the guitar. Later, he married, had nine healthy children and was a successful business man. He never returned to Greece or saw his parents again.

It is that kind of courage, desire and purpose combined with a "vision" that makes people and leaders successful. Life is filled with both joy and adversity. It is the adversity, with its accompanying obstacles, challenges and pain, which is part of life's test.

Mary Pickford, the actress and founder of United Artists, once said, "The thing we call 'failure' is not in the falling down but in the staying down."

My parents and the leaders I knew personally fell often, but they never stayed down long. They made a conscious decision to pick themselves up and ask themselves what they had learned from the experience and how they could empower themselves and their families.

I read somewhere that our spirituality, defined by how we treat ourselves and others, is directly related to our faith. Our faith comes from knowing and placing our trust in a power far greater than ourselves. Our spirituality, connected with our faith, helps us to find the thing called "inner peace." There is no magic key that unlocks the formula for life and inner peace; faith and spirituality bring leadership and quality improvement principles into focus.

It is not *if* but *how* and *when* we choose to develop and implement our spirituality and faith sequentially — inside out, not outside in.

I can still hear my mother's voice saying to me, "Everything happens for a reason and it will turn out okay. You'll see. Just don't ever quit and know that I love you."

INTRODUCTION

This book was written to help plant some "seeds" that will lead to a harvest of ideas and concepts to enhance your personal lives. Our lives are indeed fertile and holy ground. We plant the seeds of positive ideas and affirmations because we believe positive things can happen. All of us are part of the web called "life."

To make the web stronger, we can either choose right actions and right words, or we can make it weaker through wrong actions, with negative and hurtful words.

In addition to the principles and examples in the text, you will find at the end of each chapter several questions that will act as a review for that particular principle. And finally, Chapter Six, **"Values We Can Embrace"** will offer ten specific ways you can enhance your life.

Throughout the book, principles are discussed which can help you become not only a better person and leader, but will urge you to encourage others to tell you how well you are doing and what they are thinking about you. There is often a wide expanse between how we see what we are doing and how other people are seeing us. You might, for example, give yourself fairly high marks for being an effective leader because hardly anyone is disagreeing with you. Conversely, perhaps your employees, friends, and family think your actions are not reflecting your words. Of course, there is always the possibility that while you think you are really terrific, everyone else thinks you are a conceited and narrow-minded individual.

It is important that you solicit positive and constructive feedback from others. These individuals will tell you the truth, tell you what you need to know, and not what you want to hear. The type of feedback you will seek will provide you a 360 degree mirror of yourself.

This is a book designed to maximize your effectiveness as a person, whether you are a CEO, clerk, engineer, firefighter, teacher, husband, wife, student or an apprentice. We all need these principles because they are the building blocks of trust, commitment, integrity and faith.

It is my hope that this material is simple, personal, practical and enjoyable. If you can create a positive change in yourself and make it stick, then you can influence your environment, your community and your workplace; maybe even the world.

In any event, whatever your present levels of leadership skills, principles, values and faith are, and you want to make a change to improve them, you have come to the right place.

Welcome aboard!

CHAPTER 1

VALUE-CENTERED LEADERSHIP

"Popularity is the pocket change of history and courage is its true currency."

— Charlton Heston

Leadership, guiding a group of people (including yourself), is arguably the single most important role any executive fulfills as part of his or her personal and professional mission. Andrew Dubrin, in his book *A Ten Minute Guide to Leadership*, says that a vital part of being an effective leader is, "To first define leadership and what leadership encompasses."

From my personal study, efforts and musings, I discovered the term "leadership" defined in many ways. One definition is that the most successful leaders are people who know how to manage things and lead people.

Leadership is such an important topic in today's world that it has been defined in many ways by people in all walks of life and under different circumstances. Each definition contains an important message for individuals aspiring to be effective leaders or attempting to improve their personal lives.

In short, leadership involves acts of inspiring, motivating, persuading others, and being the lightning rod for meaningful change. Real, meaningful change is especially important when our country faces issues that can determine the existence of our culture and our way of life.

> **"No man will make a great leader who wants to do it himself, or to get all of the credit for doing it."**
> **—Andrew Carnegie**

The definition of leadership of which I am most fond combines the qualities espoused by President Harry S. Truman, General Dwight D. Eisenhower, and Sir Winston Churchill: Pulling people along a path they may not go themselves, making them feel good about the journey, and upon arrival, creating an environment where people believe they thought of the idea themselves. Leaders influence human behavior in an environment of uncertainty.

I attended a quality improvement seminar in Seattle, Washington in 1990 and recall what the keynote address speaker said, "Effective leaders create an environment which gives people the opportunity to contribute to the maximum extent possible. An effective leader makes the employees heroes for doing it, and lets them have fun while doing their work. In the end, the leader thanks them."

Effective leaders are also students of psychology; they study human behavior. For example, leaders must study a person's intentions, actions, emotions, and ideas. In their book *Psychology for Leaders, The Portable MBA Series*, Dean and Mary Tjosvold state that, "Leaders occupy the role of a psychologist whether they want to or not, and that role is thrust upon them simply by occupying the position of authority over other people."

Leaders must learn how to work with people and how to accomplish the organization's goals by pulling people along a path versus pushing them down a path. Most people do not want to be pushed; they want to be pulled. If you, as a leader, have people working for you who require more pushing than pulling, perhaps it is time to reevaluate your recruitment, selection, retention and promotion policies.

10

> **"If your actions inspire others to dream more, learn more, do more and become more, then you are a leader."**
> **—John Quincy Adams**

Leaders create a vision that tells their subordinates where the organization is headed and how they will get there. The "where" is a strategic perspective attained by looking five, ten, or even twenty years into the future to determine how the organization will take shape to meet its customers' and shareholders' needs and expectations. The "how" part of the vision contains the values which guide the organization on its journey. The values include: Communication, trust, integrity, customer service, and quality.

For example, General George S. Patton saw action in France during World War I. In 1942, he was assigned duty as a Major General at Desert Training Center in Indio, California. Although it was an important assignment, he was disappointed in this assignment because he wanted to be in the war raging in Europe and North Africa. Patton did not let this disappointment deter him from doing his best because he desired to be in command. In March, 1943, after participating in the landings in North Africa, he was given command of the troops which had just suffered a humiliating defeat at the hands of "The Desert Fox," under General Erwin Rommel. When General Patton arrived at his new command, he found the troops were demoralized and dispirited, and were more like a "rabble" than soldiers ready to fight.

His first step was to order the troops to wear only regulation Army uniforms, including neckties, leggings and heavy steel helmets. Patton knew that if his men felt like soldiers, they would act like soldiers. He did not tolerate sloppiness and practiced what he called his "war in the water." This simply meant that he had to lead from the front and not from behind. General Patton often said, "A leader has to be ahead of his men, you must know what is going on all the time. You cannot swim without being in the water." He knew he was fighting a war and

11

not running for political office. He had to have the courage to make unpopular decisions. However, Patton was not an autocrat either, and surrounded himself with people whose knowledge and judgment he trusted. He never launched a campaign without first reviewing the plan with his senior staff. General Patton never forced an operation down their throats, but he encouraged open and candid discussions.

To make certain he would not be caught short in a campaign, General Patton also had a Contingency Plan and said that, "Formulating a single plan and sticking to it is one-dimensional thinking. To survive and succeed, you need more than just one plan." Patton's philosophy is useful to any leadership endeavor.

With his example as a benchmark, my personal and professional experiences have consistently demonstrated seven basic effective leadership principles that are valid in almost any situation. These principles will enhance leadership effectiveness, efficiency and skill.

1) Leaders have a vision.
Effective leaders possess great Rolodexes from which to identify and surround themselves with people who complement their own skills. They know where they want to go and the types of people they need to assist them on "the journey." They base many of their recruiting, selection, and retention criteria on the type of individuals who will best fit the vision, especially individuals who are willing to commit to it themselves.

Effective leaders are also articulate. They can paint a picture of their vision and communicate it effectively. They take a structural approach, viewing the organization as a group of interconnected systems. With these interconnected systems, the leader will create the mechanisms that produce the right behaviors based on a collection of the organization's core values. The core values include: Trust, integrity, customer service, quality, teamwork, etc.

Organizational leaders must have the ability to see patterns in their organizations as if they were sitting on a balcony. They view the world from this balcony and believe they can accomplish anything through education, hard work and training. Noted writer and lecturer, Deepak Chopra said, "This is going outside the self and looking back."

> "Cherish your vision and your dreams as they are the children of your soul, the blueprints of your ultimate achievements."
> —Napoleon Hill

Effective leaders must envision a context for change. They must also provide their employees with a sense of the organization's history, and the role each person must take in order to help shape the organization's future. Effective leaders know that the whole is the sum of its parts and any organization is only as strong as its weakest link; an effective leader can identify that link.

Effective leaders explore the innate emotions that help them become more insightful and intuitive about the processes involved, as well as the people around them. For example, Walt Disney was recognized as an effective "animator" because he knew the type of talent he needed to help him achieve his vision. Steve Jobs, the founder of Apple Computer, did not have just ideas, but insanely great ideas and the vision to go along with them. He wanted people with the same vision.

What matters is that you know where you are going, how you are going to get there, and if you are articulating it to others. It's important to know the "how to's" or you will just be another empty suit.

> "Whenever you see a successful business, someone once made courageous decisions."
> —Peter Drucker

2) *Leaders have the courage to live their convictions.*

Effective leaders are accountable and are not afraid to make unpopular decisions. Historically, our country has been led by people who knew what needed to be done and who were not swayed by popular or unpopular opinion. For example, Abraham Lincoln was forced to engage our country in its most damaging and disruptive war instead of permitting the South to secede from the Union. If the South had been allowed to secede, the United States as we know it may have ceased to exist.

> **"Whenever I make a bum decision, I just go out and make another."**
> **—President Harry Truman**

During the Berlin Airlift in the winter of 1948, all of President Truman's advisors encouraged him to stop the airlift. They were concerned that the snow, fog and poor visibility would significantly increase the risk of airplane disasters to U.S. air crews. President Truman knew that if he had given orders to terminate the airlift of food and medical supplies to the occupied city of Berlin, not only would thousands of people have starved, but it would have drastically changed the world's political environment and our country's role in it. Truman knew what had to be done and refused to cancel the airlift. When he left office, his popularity was at a low thirty-two percent. Today, he is recognized as one of this country's greatest presidents of the 20th Century.

3) *Leaders Walk the Talk.*

Effective leaders have their specific points of view and are not afraid to express them. When confronted with difficult decisions or political correctness, leaders do not waffle or raise an index finger to gauge the prevailing political winds. They base their decisions on what is right and honorable for the country, state or organization and not what is politically correct or expedient.

Effective leaders have the ability to inspire trust and confidence in the people with whom they work. Once leaders make a decision, they do not change their mind in midstream; they possess the flexibility to change a decision if extreme circumstances dictate that a change is necessary. They encourage open and candid dialogue among employees to improve a process or policy. They empower their people to learn how and when to share the power.

Effective leaders have the personal courage to disclose their own shortcomings and to admit they can not do it alone. In so doing, they become vulnerable and human. They create an environment where it is safe for people to vent their frustration and where they are able to deliver an unpopular or unwelcomed message; understanding that the leader will not "shoot the messenger."

Their actions must reflect their words. Stated another way, leaders "walk–the-talk" instead of merely "talking–the-talk."

4) Leaders have positive self-expression.
I have heard it said that "people who succeed speak well of themselves to themselves." They make positive self-talk an integral part of their lives, filling themselves with positive affirmations about who they are and where they are going, often resulting in positive outcomes.

> **"If anything is within the powers and province of man, believe that it is within your own compass also."**
> **—Marcus Aurelius**

Effective leaders convey to others through thought, word and deed that they believe in them. The saying, "If you want others to believe in you, you must first convince them you believe in them," is true. Kevin Cashman, a Minneapolis, Minnesota-based leadership coach and consultant, calls this leadership attribute "positive self-expression"; it is more than just "straight talk." He says, "Authentic self-expression goes beyond telling the truth. It demonstrates a total congruence between who you are and what you do and say."

Leaders make so many positive statements about being successful that other individuals start believing in the leader's self-confidence. At the same time, these individuals also begin to believe in themselves.

5) *Leaders manage by walking around–outside.*

The truly great leaders view themselves as "people growers," when they provide opportunities for people to learn and grow spiritually, personally and professionally. They know that valid growth is sequential; personal growth happens from the inside out, not the outside in. While on the job, they implement MBWA–O (Management by Walking Around–Outside) an important process by which they conduct business.

> **"Tell them quick. Tell them often." —
> William Wrigley, Jr.**

In 1992, I attended a leadership quality improvement seminar at the Sir Frances Drake Hotel in Chicago, Illinois. The keynote address speaker asked the audience, "Do you want to know if your leader is committed to change?" Suddenly, all 600 or so people in the audience became quiet. It was as if our collective minds had become one as we thought about her question. After giving us a few seconds to contemplate what she had just asked us, she responded. "Check their day planner," she said. "If it is filled with meetings and appointments, they are spending too much time in the office behind the desk. If it is open, your leader is spending more time outside the office, walking around the organization and visiting with the people."

16

For example, Mr. Orville Merillat, founder of Merillat Industries in Adrian, Michigan spent most of his time out in the plant, notebook in hand, walking around checking on production and visiting with his employees. This habit enabled Mr. Merillat to determine if the company was meeting its production quotas and getting to know his employees and their families on a first name basis. During his daily tours, he also took the time asking questions and listening to the employee's feedback.

Do you spend most of your day in your office hiding behind your desk, or are you making it a habit by walking around meeting people at their work sites?

6) Leaders are made, not born.

Effective leaders have become great because they climbed over obstacles that would have stopped most other people. It was Aristotle who said, "Leadership is not an art, it is a habit." Effective leaders view the obstacles as simply another one of life's teachable moments that will help them grow as a person. Throughout history, great leaders' personal and professional histories chronicle who they are and what they have accomplished; they are truly inspirational. They are survivors in the truest sense of the word. They live their lives with a simple common philosophy, "Never give up, and never give up, never, never, never give up!"

> **"Change before you have to."**
> **—Jack Welch**

Is the leader aware of the need to change and able to take the steps necessary to change personally and professionally? Or is he or she a "hack" or a "gofer" for other people, who never had an original idea themselves and who wait for someone else to make a decision and then try to take credit for it? As we deal with each new challenge, we unleash an internal power in ourselves, freeing our capacity to soar to new heights.

7) *Leaders have integrity.*

Webster's Collegiate Dictionary defines integrity as, "Strict personal honesty and independence; completeness; unity; soundness." Integrity is the whole you, it is the sum of everything you are at any given time in your life. It is your character, honor and courage. You have integrity when your actions mirror your words. It is that internal anchor and value that provides you with the courage to stand and defend that which you believe.

> **"One's integrity can give a person something to rely on when perspective seems to blur, when rules seem to waiver, and when faced with a hard choice of right and wrong. A clear conscience is one's only protection."**
> **—Admiral James B. Stockdale**

Writer and consultant, George Shapiro, earned a Ph.D. and became a professor at the University of Minnesota, specializing in Organizational and Leadership Communications. A consultant to several Fortune 500 companies, Mr. Shapiro believes integrity is the single most important attribute in effective leadership and personal success. He states that integrity has three basic core values: first, you do not lie; second, you do not withhold information from people with whom you work; and third, you do not preach one thing and then do another. The definition of integrity that I like is "what a person does when no one else is around."

The essence of leadership can be summed up by the following quote I read on a plaque. It stated: "A true leader has the confidence to stand alone, the courage to make tough decisions and the compassion to listen to the needs of others. He does not set out to be a leader, but becomes one by the quality of his actions and the integrity of his intent. In the end, leaders are much like eagles; they do not flock, and you find them one at a time."

Thinking Points about Leadership:
- Do you pull from the front or push from behind?
- Do you try to swim without getting into the water?
- Do you have a vision? What is it?
- What are your convictions? Do you stick to them?
- What fears are preventing you from reaching your goals?
- Do your actions mirror your words?
- Do you sit behind your desk most of the day or do you visit and interact with your employees?

CHAPTER 2

TAKING CHARGE OF CHANGE

"Life is hard by the yard; but a cinch by the inch."
—Author Unknown

Change has many different meanings and like its related term, quality, it is a continuous process. To be successful, all meaningful change must be sequential; it starts on the inside and not the outside. Change can be simple and straightforward. We can either choose to embrace it and make it our ally, or we can resist it. If we make the conscious choice to resist it, then we become part of the problem and not part of the solution. But, if we make the conscious choice to embrace change, then we become part of the solution.

> **"Change is not made without inconvenience, even from worse to better."**
> **—Richard Hooker**

Anyone who has ever set a goal to change their attitude and their behavior has discovered that it takes great effort. People who want to change will need to spend much energy in order to focus on the issues that will help them make the change happen. These same individuals also need to have confidence in their leaders and know that their leaders are committed to the change. I think most individuals will commit to, if not totally enroll in, the change process when their performance and contributions encourage them to do so. Most people must be given a legitimate reason, or an external stimulus, which will encourage them to change and accept the results of the change. Therefore, leaders must ensure that the employee's job performance is directly related to that individual's willingness to acquire new skills, and to establish new relationships. Meaningful, long-lasting change will not occur if the above steps are not implemented.

"Change and the uncertainty it brings is accelerating," says Dallas, Texas consultant Price Pritchett. "The more change and the faster it comes at us, the easier it is for us to get blindsided."

There are individuals who have an intrinsic need to function within a fixed structure where they rely on others to tell them what to do and how to do it. This, I believe, is learned behavior.

Conversely, there are others who thrive in a flexible and fluid environment. They have learned to take control of their lives and are self-motivators. It is easier for these individuals to shine in a less formal structure; in other words, they make a conscious choice to shine instead of whine.

I have often wondered if there is some type of genetic code at work in these situations. How else can this mind-set be explained in the divergent and varied behaviors of the folks who always see the glass half-full instead of half-empty? I believe all of us can improve our willingness and ability to deal with change and the uncertainty that usually follows. The only way we really know how to respond is to face a valid yet uncertain set of circumstances which test our personal and professional values.

It is important to mention that, as with any change mechanism, an organization may see some initial results of its efforts to implement the change process. However, practical experience has revealed that any meaningful change requires from three to five years before the change takes hold and becomes part of the organization's culture.

In his book, *The Dance of Change: The Challenges to Sustaining Momentum in Learning Organizations*, Peter Senge states, "Companies are actually organisms, not machines, and that might explain why it's so difficult for us to succeed in our efforts to produce change." He explains that when change is implemented within an organization, the leader hires "mechanics" when what really is needed are "gardeners." In other words, leaders must begin learning how to be gardeners by planting ideas instead of thinking that everything or everyone needs fixing.

Richard Russell, Director of Corporate Strategy Development at the U. S. Navy's Undersea Warfare Center (NUWC) in Newport, Rhode Island, calls his role at NUWC, "Chief Irritant and Instigator." His job is to challenge and "irritate" the Center employees who hold onto obsolete ways of thinking. He develops ways to instigate and initiate breakthroughs about the future of the Navy's technology and fighting capabilities. This process challenges employees to spend less time thinking about what worked in the past and spend more time asking about what can be done in the future.

Russell initiated a process he terms the "thinking expedition." It encourages individuals to think about change, tap into an individual's creativity by defining what a thinking expedition does and how the expedition is doing it. One "thinking expedition" employs a scenario built around a hurricane which sweeps through Newport, destroying every building on the base and killing all but 50 inhabitants. In the model, those people who are still alive have a mission to organize the reconstruction of the base. Questions such as, "Where should we rebuild the facilities and put the base?" and, "What facilities are critical" are posed to employees in order to challenge them to think critically. The logic behind these types of questions and other types of exercises

> **"Nothing great is created suddenly, any more than a bunch of grapes or a fig. Let it first blossom, then bear fruit, then ripen."**
> **—Epictetus**

is to shock people into thinking about the organization's mission. Why it exists and what is its real contribution to the Navy and to the community at large?

Russell encouraged his people to express their thoughts and ideas on three by five cards he called "blue slips." As a result of this expression, the blue slips used in the hurricane exercise generated hundreds of ideas about the center's blind spots and its potential for the future. Russell said, "People unzipped their foreheads."

Therefore, what organizations need are many more "seed carriers." It is similar to farmers who plant seeds in the ground to grow new crops. Organizations need people who know how to "plant seeds" to encourage dialogue and to find ways to work for the good of the whole—in other words, planters. We need fewer "spear carriers," those individuals who sit back and blame others, and more individuals who are ready to work for the good of the whole. The leader can cultivate willing relationships which are more gratifying than struggling to salvage those that were not meant to be.

Committing to meaningful change is an approach you can choose to take, and it is the difference between wondering what happened, wishing something would happen, or making something happen.

Taking charge of change requires that you take the initiative to improvise and experiment to see what works and what does not work, and talk among yourselves. It can be stated another way: Improvise, act; improvise, act, and improvise!

I have often heard individuals ask, "Why should I endure learning a new behavior unless I can see that there is something in it for me?" Or, "How can I have trust and have confidence in our leaders if they are unable or lack the will to help me understand my contributions to the big picture?"

Douglas K. Smith writes in *Taking Charge of Change*, "If leaders aspire to change, they must help people connect their efforts to the big picture." When people see that leaders are truly committed to and enrolled in the change process, it enhances their confidence in the leader's ability to lead them on the journey.

Employees monitor every aspect of their leaders' attitude and behavior; they watch, listen, and draw mental pictures to create their own version of who is in charge. More importantly, people watch how leaders conduct their lives. Are they really believing in the concept of change or are they keeping it at arms length, thinking and acting as if it is for everyone else but not for themselves? More than words, pictures and initiatives, your actions tell a lot about what you truly believe and what you are most likely to do. What you do in the hallway is more important than what you say in the conference room. For that reason, your words and actions must be unified.

> **"The exact words you use are far less important than the energy, intensity and conviction with which you use them."**
> **—Jules Rose**

For example, I led a course in Strategic Planning as an adjunct faculty member at Ottawa University in Kansas City. An important part of the course requirement included a project to be selected by the adult learners and to be related directly to the mission and goals of the course. During one of the class sessions, an adult learner discussed his company's attempt to change the organization's culture and implement a "Change Management Process." The company where he was employed at the time was well-known throughout the Midwest for producing food products, fertilizers and related farming materials. The company's Chief Executive Officer (CEO) suggested a "dress-down day" as one of the first steps in the change process. It was decided by the CEO and his senior staff that all employees would be permitted to come to work one day dressed in western clothing. A few days later, teams of employees prepared and posted announcements heralding the dress-down day and were anxiously waiting for the day to arrive. Everyone was excited that the usual dress code requirements were being relaxed and a number of people thought that maybe their boss was really serious about making a change this time. The day arrived and men wore blue jeans, western shirts, and cowboy boots; and women wore western skirts, boots, blouses, and related apparel. Though they were busily working, most of the employees consciously or subconsciously were waiting to see what the CEO would wear that morning. Well, guess what? A few minutes after the start of the "dress-down day," the CEO entered the building wearing a suit and tie. The news of his apparel that morning spread throughout the corporate headquarters like a Midwestern prairie grass fire. The employees' perception of his attitude towards them was validated by that one act; now they knew he believed that change was for everyone else but him.

From that point on, any attempt the CEO made to talk about "change" or "quality improvement" was subtly resisted and the employees chuckled among themselves. "He just didn't get it!" The adult learner said, "He just didn't get it! He expected everyone else to do it but thought it was beneath him to dress-down."

The lesson learned in this example is that in order to become an effective role model you must make a commitment to keeping your word; keeping your word says much about who you are as a person. This attitude, in turn, begins to build more confidence in yourself and confidence in the people around you.

All meaningful change starts with an honest, objective decision to look inside yourself to determine your strengths, weaknesses or challenges. Any change will not work if you are not willing to honestly look at who you are, where you are going, and what strategy you are using to get there. People not only look at your actions when you define a vision; they also peer into the whole you. They are looking at your character to determine if your personal vision includes the courage, commitment and confidence to change yourself. Do your actions match your words or is it simply more forms over substance--fluff and no stuff?

In other words, effective leaders learn how to assertively "communicate, communicate, and communicate" so they are able to connect with their employees. Transformational leaders are like actors and teachers; they continually repeat their lines to any audience they can find. They interpret their vision and mission for anyone who will listen.

Assertive communication is like pitching a baseball game. You must have an overall strategy for pitching your point of view and learning not to focus solely on your own desires to the extent you forget to focus on your opponent's goals and objectives. Effective communicators identify what their opponents want, and then try to predict how their opponents will respond. While every prediction may not result in 100% success, over time this strategy will improve your chances for success, and you will end up winning more than you will lose.

> **"Noise proves nothing. Often a hen who has merely laid an egg cackles as if she laid an asteroid."** **—Mark Twain**

Communicating change or other major issues face-to-face is the only way to do it; videos, publications, or large meetings are not as effective.

Once the strategy for implementing meaningful change is designed, the most difficult part is clearing the next hurdle; that being the employee's resistance to it. The leader may have a "can't-miss-program," and may have arranged for senior level support, commitment and sponsorship. This does not matter because experience shows that the organization's mid-level managers and front-line employees will resist all of your best-laid plans. Some will fight them openly, but many more will work behind the scenes to sabotage them. The leader's best effort for implementing change will prove fruitless if the leader does not have an effective strategy for getting people committed and enrolled in the change process.

According to consultant Mark Maletz, the reason that most people resist any kind of change is that they do not viscerally understand what is in it for them; their experience has demonstrated that any type of change is seldom for the better. If you have been with an organization for any length of time, and you have seen any number of "the flavor-of-the-month" change programs come and go, you quickly begin to recognize a pattern. Leadership launches some kind of change effort with great fanfare. The managers start to verbalize the benefits of the way this particular effort will be good for the company and its employees. Maletz says, "They make all the requisite promises, but at the end of the day they fail to deliver. On reflection, you realize that it was much ado about nothing; and the entire effort seemed like a complete waste of time, money, resources and energy."

There is a more insidious kind of hostility that occurs when a consultant visits the organization and determines that less people are needed to do a specific job. If you are in the department that is earmarked for down-sizing, one of two things will probably happen. 1) Either you will lose your job, or, 2) you will stay and work even harder. So, there really is a history in many organizations that basically say, "Our efforts at change in the past have not been good. There is no reason for you to believe that it will be anything different this time, either."

Maletz said, "You can expect some hostility towards your plan, it is rarely the in-your-face kind of resistance. The resistance is usually passive-aggressive, meaning it is usually deeply underground and behind your back. It is a kind of hostility that is harder to overcome." People will listen to you and say nothing that is overtly negative, but in their minds, they do not really commit to, and enroll in, your change process. As soon as they are alone with their peers, they usually say something like, "We have seen this all before. It is just another program our bosses are trying so they can look good to their bosses. This will pass just like all the other efforts, so we will wait this one out, too." Historically, their rationale is usually right because any impact the change is supposed to affect never goes very deep into the organization — and when it does, the results are usually counter-productive.

The grassroots' leaders will not hesitate to let you know if they see a problem with the change process. If they do see a problem, you must find a way to win them over.

Start this process by cultivating relationships with people by inviting them to engage in meaningful dialogue with you. Invite them into your office or meet away from their work area. You are not trying to make a "sales pitch," but you are trying to engage in meaningful conversation -- exchanging ideas -- a "talking through," which is the definition of dialogue. In this way, you are offering them a symbolic contract and a meaningful role in the process, signifying that you want them to become a voice for the change process. It is important that you make it clear to them that you are listening to their constructive criticisms and that you are making every effort to respond to them in some way.

> **"Men are never so likely to settle a question rightly as when they discuss it freely."**
> **—Thomas Babington**

Being up front is the most effective and efficient strategy regarding change. Tell employees exactly what it is you want to do and call it by that name. For example, when organizations tried to claim that re-engineering was not about down-sizing, they wondered why their people became angry and negative. The re-engineering efforts were, in fact, all about down-sizing and leaders refusing to tell everyone up front that some employees were going to lose their jobs. It is as if they did not think their employees would be able to figure that out on their own until it was too late.

Mark Maletz was involved in a change effort to make a high-tech, major industrial organization more entrepreneurial. He said, "An employee stood up and said that we had totally missed the fact that there was no way to find critical resources for entrepreneurial ventures in this organization." As a result of the criticism, the organization created an internal clearinghouse that identified employees' functional specialties, so when the specialties were needed, they could quickly be found.

Although it sounds like an oxymoron, change is a constant force in our personal and professional lives. Generally, we can handle the minor ones almost without thinking by shifting speeds as we drive our automobile down the chosen highway of life.

Questions to ask ourselves:
- How do we handle the major changes?
- How do we handle the life-changing and life-altering processes?
- How do we address the major detours and roadblocks?
- How do we react when the lane suddenly stops and we are on cruise control, or the accelerator pedal sticks or our automobile no longer moves-forward?
- What should we do and how should we act when the change strikes us at the core of our beliefs—destroying our habits, throwing us into a state of panic and confusion, and challenging our self-esteem like never before?

This situation occurs when something or someone threatens to take away our livelihood. Metaphorically, this can be called our "food" — which is any source of fulfillment — a belief, a relationship, or a habit of doing a certain thing at a certain time every day for years. The "food" in this example is your job and the organization that feeds you, or you are facing a life threatening injury, illness or personal loss.

> **"Great crises produce great men and great deeds of courage."** —John F. Kennedy

My parents, like many of their peers, held the same jobs for almost their entire lives; that was the way things were in most communities 30 to 40 years ago. When I graduated from college in 1963, the prevailing wisdom of the time was that you would have three major jobs in a lifetime. Today, with down-sizing and the volatility that comes with it, it is best to plan on seven or more job changes. Some of the changes are the employees' choice and some are the results of down-sizing and lay-offs. Regardless of the reason, seven jobs are a lot in one lifetime.

When a job loss or something even more difficult occurs, you can choose to use your instinct, abilities and confidences to confront the situation. Look for new "food," or you can wail, rage and delude yourself into thinking that some new food will somehow magically appear. Job loss or another of life's many challenges is about taking charge of the change in your life and viewing the change as yet another adventure to be experienced. This challenge is one of the major differences between a victim and a survivor; both individuals experience grief and the loss of an identity. But grieving will not bring back the food and that understanding quickly dawns on the survivor. The victim chooses to remain static -- physically, emotionally and spiritually -- and wallows in his or her loss. They mount their "pity-potty" early and stay there, often for years. Being a victim becomes their symbol of repression, shabby treatment and how unfair life (and the organization) has been to them. They refuse to listen to their beliefs or lose them along the way, choosing instead to focus their energies on themselves and not the bigger picture. They remain angry at the hand they have been dealt; they curse the lemons and discard them instead of trying to make lemonade.

> **"The man who complains about the way the ball bounces is probably the one who dropped it."** —Lou Holtz

The survivor begins to consider the world that is outside of their comfort zone and is the first to question, evaluate and adjust his or her beliefs. If a person believes that the next step will be met with disappointment and rejection, that person will never move forward and never change; things will remain as they are now. Many people have been programmed to believe that change, by its very name, is inherently negative. According to spiritual counselor and author, Adele Tartaglia, "Most people fear change when in fact, change can be a blessing from God. It allows you to create your own life." The survivor also makes a conscious decision to stop majoring in the minors. It is important to stop worrying about every little thing that happens.

When a major change occurs, it challenges your belief systems because it forces you to re-examine what is important, who you are, where you need to go and how you plan to get there. Suddenly, that which you thought was important becomes secondary and maybe not even on your radar screens at all. Acting on your decision means making a commitment and preparing to embark on another adventure. On this new journey, old cultures, old habits and old ways of thinking are discarded. In their place, you become open to change and you allow the experiences of the moment to unfold before you one of life's "teachable moments" -- you find out what (and who) you have been taking for granted -- perhaps for most of your life.

True and valid change does not exist without taking risks. Survivors, like effective leaders, are not afraid to be vulnerable and are able to admit that they do not know it all and that they can not do it alone. The risks that are taken and how they are handled can educate the traveler. One of life's universal lessons is that individuals, regardless of their station or position in life, can wake-up one morning and discover that their "food" has been moved.

> **"Only those who will risk going too far can possibly find out how far one can go."**
> **—T. S. Eliot**

You can get off to a good start by understanding what you want to change, why you want to change, and select only issues that are worth your effort to clearly visualize your goals. Establish an objective and do first things first, the rest of the process will follow. The key to continuous improvement is the understanding of the process of change. This process includes recognizing the need for change, then empowering yourself to change.

> **"When you reach for the stars, you may not quite get them, but you won't come up with a handful of mud either."**
> **—Leo Burnett**

The ancient Greeks had a saying, "Well begun: half-done."

As with most other issues in life, if you are really serious about change, you will find the means, methods, and desires to change; this means you must make the commitment to Walk-the-Talk. It is simply having your actions mirror your words.

Thinking Points about Change.
- Do you embrace change and make it an ally or do you resist it?
- Do you conduct regular "thinking expeditions" with yourself and your team, or do you hold onto obsolete ways of thinking?
- Are you a "planter" or a "spear thrower"?
- Do you have a passionate commitment to a cause, or do you sleepwalk through life?

CHAPTER 3

THE OMEGA LEADER

"Where there is no vision, the people will perish."
— Proverbs 18:29

In the book, *Jesus CEO*, Laurie Beth Jones outlines three unique styles of leadership. Maybe you have heard of them and pattern your style of leadership using one of the concepts. If you have not, here is a review of the three leadership styles discussed in her book: The Alpha Style of leadership is based on the masculine, authoritative, autocratic style of power while the Beta Style of leadership is based on the feminine, cooperative use of power. The Omega Leadership Style incorporates and enhances both the Alpha and Beta styles of leadership.

This Omega Leadership Style was the concept used by Jesus as He trained twelve human beings to follow Him. Jesus' twelve disciples were so thoroughly trained in His Omega style of leadership that they continued to influence the world long after His recorded time on Earth. In studying Jesus' leadership techniques, Laurie Beth Jones says that Jesus, the original Omega leader, had three essential powers:

- The strength of self-mastery
- The strength of action
- The strength of relationships

As a leader, you may have only one or two of these characteristics, but truly great leaders have all three.

This man, Jesus of Nazareth, a simple carpenter, worked with people who were far from being divine, but human beings who were just like you and me. They had their own reasons and agendas for wanting to join Him. They often fought among themselves in their attempt to get closer to Jesus and to be rewarded for following Him. They were even overtaken with momentary cowardice; we all know the story of one "employee"

> **"Leadership is based on a spiritual quality – the power to inspire, the power to inspire others to follow."**
> **—Vince Lombardi**

who turned against his leader for thirty pieces of silver.

Regardless of all the personal and political agendas among His "team," Jesus trained and empowered His disciples to do the work they were trained to do. Their reason for doing so was simple – being with Him in paradise.

Jesus' Omega leadership style was also intended to be used by us in our daily lives. Jesus CEO has a powerful yet obvious message. Effective leaders benchmark these qualities for the kinds of disciples they want on their team and create the specific requirements for recruiting, selecting, training, and retaining them. In order to successfully implement these processes, they are more likely to secure "followership" from their employees as Jesus did with His apostles. The leader's vision and mission are, by their very nature, created to weed out the loners, curmudgeons and the individuals who do not really believe in the direction the organization is headed and how it will get there.

Any knowledge, skill, or ability you want people to learn can be learned. The presumption is that people, as part of their overall personal strategy, possess the innate drive and desire to learn a little more about themselves and their job every day. They view life-long learning as a continual process and take responsibility for their own career management.

Curiosity, initiative, and collegiality, which are the

> **"To teach is to learn twice."**
> **—Piet Joubert**

qualities of disciples and effective self-directed teams, however, are not teachable. These traits are inherent in an individual's attitude and must be ascertained before a candidate is hired.

In *D-Day the 6th of June*, David Ambrose discusses how the Supreme Allied Commander General Dwight David Eisenhower faced not only difficult and stressful military decisions but political decisions as well. Eisenhower's decisions literally affected the lives of thousands of Americans and allied serviceman.

Eisenhower's tasks were made even more daunting because he needed to balance daily his military knowledge with the competing political factions. For example, during the initial planning stages of the Normandy Invasion, because they were concerned about the higher than expected loss of life, a large number of his staff were against dropping airborne troops behind the German lines. The mission of the airborne troops was quite specific: "To interdict the German lines of communications, delay German counterattacks and destroy specific bridges." Without this type of tactical attack, General Eisenhower knew the troops landing on the Normandy Beachhead would be in peril, placing the entire invasion in serious jeopardy. If that occurred, he knew the Allies would face their own "Dunkirk." As it turned out, the loss of human life, especially on Omaha Beach, was still quite high but within acceptable limits in a battle of that magnitude. Imagine the loss of life if General Eisenhower had listened to members of his staff and not approved the insertion of airborne troops a few miles behind German lines.

General Eisenhower knew what needed to be done and had confidence and faith in his ability to make the tough decisions. He was full of resolve and refused to entertain any doubts. When he planned the Normandy Invasion with his staff, he did not permit any "provideds," only "challenges," with his staff. On January 23, 1943, he told his superiors, the Combined Chiefs of Staff (CCS), "Every obstacle must be overcome, every inconvenience suffered and every risk run to ensure that our blow is decisive. We cannot afford to fail."

As a result of his training at West Point, his related military schools and his staff positions, Eisenhower had all the necessary professional credentials. He knew what it took to succeed and was determined that no one would deter him from accomplishing his mission. General Eisenhower also possessed another important quality besides his aptitude, his philosophy was to never quit. He expressed this over and over again to his staff and the troops under his command. He knew the war had to be won. If the Allies did not prevail, the outcome would be too gruesome to imagine.

> **"Defensive strategy never has produced ultimate victory."**
> **—General Douglas MacArthur**

In addition to the political factions he dealt with, General Eisenhower and the men under his command also were facing inclement and rapidly changing weather. Because of weather, high tides and other factors, the landings on the Normandy Beaches were a debacle. The 1999 movie, *Saving Private Ryan*, is a fairly accurate depiction of the Allies' landing and of the chaos American soldiers and their allies faced against a well-fortified and entrenched German army. Many American officers were killed either immediately after leaving their landing craft or on the beaches a few minutes after landing. Lower ranking enlisted men and even some privates took command and began to oversee the strategy, tactics and communicating with the other teams on the beaches. The soldiers' survival was directly related to their inner desire to live. This innate drive to live was related to the grittiness of many Americans of that era. The soldiers knew what needed to be done and did not have the time or the inclination to seek approval for advancing from the beachhead from the command structure moored in boats off shore. Driven by their

> **"The secret of discipline is motivation. When a man is sufficiently motivated, discipline will take care of itself."**
> **—Albert Einstein**

innate need to survive, the soldiers formed squads on their own, created their own objectives and looked out for each other.

About ten years ago, I had a conversation with an acquaintance who lives in Europe. I met him at a seminar in Washington, D.C. and remain in touch with him periodically. During that first meeting, I recall him saying to me, "You Americans really know how to get things done." He continued to say that once we identify our mission and goals, we get organized and get them accomplished. We do not get all bogged down in playing "King of the Mountain." He added, "In my country, people get too involved in the minutiae, squabble over the details and cannot seem to agree to agree." His comments point out one of the valuable assets for teams and that is to agree to agree.

There are individuals who choose goals and start to pursue

> **"It does not matter how slowly you go as long as you do not stop."**   **—Confucius**

them before they take the time to define their vision, mission and values. Consequently, they reach the top rung of the ladder, and often discover to their dismay that the ladder is leaning against the wrong wall.

An effective vision has many of the following characteristics:

- It is simple and concise, usually less than 30 words.

- Visions contain a small number of clear, easily remembered aspirations.

- It is sound. Visions must be credible and grounded in strategy.

- It envisions a positive picture of the future. It speaks to the heart and the head.

- It is performance driven and answers the question, "Why are we doing this?"

- It is meaningful, powered by words or concepts that have the potential to generate meaningful interpretations that guide what—and what not—to do.

- It is inclusive. Visions must also encompass customers, suppliers, shareholders and others who matter to the organization's future.

At this point, you are probably asking, "What vision or mission statement could conceivably meet most or all of these criteria?"

Here are some examples of effective vision and mission statements:

Pfizer:

"OUR PURPOSE: We at Pfizer dedicate ourselves to helping humanity and delivering exceptional financial performance by discovering, developing and providing innovative health care products that lead to healthier and more productive lives.

OUR VALUES: To fulfill and achieve our mission, we abide by the enduring values that are the foundation of our business: Integrity; Innovation; Respect for People; Customer Focus; Teamwork; Leadership; Performance; Community."

Note: Each of the above values is explained in detail in Pfizer's corporate publications and at their web site.

DUNN-EDWARDS CORPORATION:

"We, the employees of Dunn-Edwards are:

ENERGIZED to outperform our competitors in growing sales and improving our financial performance.

SUPPORTIVE of our fellow employees, communities, and the environment.

OBSESSED with providing reliable, innovative and unparalled products and services.

PASSIONATE about meeting our customers needs so that Dunn–Edwards is always their #1 choice."

CANADIAN-PACIFIC HOTELS (ROYAL YORK HOTEL—TORONTO, CANADA):

"We will earn the loyalty of our guests by consistently exceeding their expectations for personal service and warm hospitality by welcoming them in distinctive surroundings." (Authors note: I had the opportunity to stay at the Royal York Hotel in November, 1992. It exceeded my expectations.)

RAYCHEM CORPORATION:

A Facilities Group that repairs toilets and air conditioners: "To make people feel good, to lift people's spirits through beauty, cleanliness, functionality, enthusiasm, good cheer and excellence."

EMBASSY SUITES HOTEL, (BILTMORE FASHION PARK, PHOENIX, ARIZONA):

GUEST SERVICES: WOWS! By Creating An Atmosphere Of Excitement And Surprise, We Will Provide Wildly Outrageous Wonderful Service That Inspires The Senses And Fulfills Even The Unexpected Needs Of Our Guests And Team Members WOWS!

THE AUTHOR:

"To pass the salt and make a difference in all that I choose to do, through faith, integrity, communications, respect and quality. To live each day like it is my last, and treat my family, friends and clients as I want to be treated. To give hugs!"

Get Started Now!

Write your own. Take a legal sized pad of lined paper, get a number 2 pencil, a cold glass of milk, some Oreo cookies (chocolate chip cookies work, too), sit in a comfortable chair, and begin writing your vision. Do not concern yourself with what you write; just start writing whatever comes to your mind regardless of how silly or foolish it may sound to you. Editing your vision can be done later. It is important to capture everything you dream of doing right here. No thought or idea should be omitted.

"An eternal trait of men is the need for vision and the readiness to follow it; and if men are not given the right vision, they will follow wandering fires," said Sir Richard Livingstone.

> **"Success or failure is often determined on the drawing board." —Robert J. McKain**

According to management guru, Peter Drucker, "The best way to predict the future is to create it. Once you know your vision, mission and goals that is the time to get down to doing it."

In almost every endeavor it is that way. Writers must sit down and write; speakers must speak, trainers must train, salespeople must sell, teachers must teach, painters must paint, managers must manage, and leaders must lead. Too often though, people get locked into habits that are non-productive and prevent them from moving ahead. People make living in the past a habit by looking in the rear view mirror of their lives. They invent excuses, they procrastinate, they blame others, and they doodle in the margins of life's tablet instead of seeking to write their signature boldly. So, don't be so quick to give up on your dreams but instead begin to pursue them with passion and energy and — fun.

Remember:

Conceive it. Perceive it. Achieve it. Believe it.

Thinking Points about Organizational Self-Management

- Do you have a vision? What is it?
- Are you willing to be vulnerable?
- What do you see differently—something that can or must be changed?
- Do you challenge your "Business as usual attitude"?
- What would your people answer if asked, "What is your job"? And more importantly, "Why is your job significant"?
- Do you clearly and continuously communicate to your staff the higher purpose for their activities?
- Do you play "King of the Mountain"?

CHAPTER 4

MOTIVATION IS NOT DIFFICULT— but it does take effort

"The optimist is as often wrong as the pessimist, but he is far happier."
—2001 Ways to Cheer Yourself Up

We are all part of a system – a political and economic system or a personal and professional system. If we choose to function illegally and unethically within a system, then we fail and the larger system is affected. The intrinsic knowledge that we play a role in this thing called "life" is, or should be, sufficient motivation for us to function legally, morally and ethically. Knowing that we have a purpose in life and therefore a reason for which to strive helps us become more motivated. In addition, we all must continue to have a passionate hope that we can, and do, make a difference in other people's lives.

Motivation is defined as, "A force or influence; that act of being motivated to provide a need to cause a person to act."

Although the leader's role in an organization is important, the leader cannot take the place of an individual's responsibility and accountability. I believe that most people, by their nature, are not naturally self-starters and actually make a conscious choice not to be motivated. However, persons who consciously accept the responsibility for their choices and the results of those choices increase their chances for personal happiness and professional success.

> **"The first man gets the oyster; the second man gets the shell." —Andrew Carnegie**

I am reminded of the story about the starfish. After a particularly severe storm along the coast, a man was walking along the beach looking at the various things the storm had washed up on shore. Scattered all along the beach were hundreds of starfish which were washed up on the beach by the waves and surf.

As he continued to walk along the beach, he noticed a young girl ahead of him stop every few feet and pick up a starfish and throw it back into the ocean. The man was completely puzzled by her actions so he approached the girl and asked, "Why are you throwing the starfish back into the ocean? You can not possibly make a difference to what happens to them."

As she picked up the next starfish, the young girl replied, "I've made a difference for this one, and this one, and this one," and continued to pick up a starfish and return it to its ocean home.

The young girl was motivated by a larger purpose in her life. If she made a difference to even one starfish, then that knowledge provided her the incentive and the motivation to continue her mission.

She made it her mission to continue to help the starfish to live and flourish, not to suffer and then die on a beach.

> **"A life is not important except in the impact it has on other lives."**
> **—Jackie Robinson**

And just like that young girl on the beach, we all come into contact with starfish, people who, with our assistance, can either flourish or perish.

The most successful organizations and individuals make motivation part of their daily, weekly and monthly habits; thereby

46

enhancing their chances of meeting or exceeding their stated goals and objectives.

Motivation is a habit for Kara Dowers, Vice President of Designs On You Incorporated, a Kansas City, Kansas, based women's apparel line. According to Dowers, "Businesses that make motivation a daily, weekly, and monthly habit will meet goals and raise production levels." Her approach is to motivate the company's employees so they may recognize their abilities and find their "hidden talents."

Ms. Dowers also suggests that the CEO must also set the tone of the business. It is important to establish the type of positive culture which enhances an individual's ability and willingness to take calculated risks without the fear of being chastised or terminated.

Bruce Jenner, the 1976 Olympic decathlon winner, scored 8,617 points and broke the world record for that event. An integral part of his training was to make it a habit to psych himself to believe that every single action he took would make a difference between his winning and losing. He said, "Every morning I awoke with a sense of mission, with the attitude that life had handed me a gift on that particular day, and my job was to make the most of every second."

> **"Believe deep down in your heart that you're destined to do great things."**
> **—Joe Paterno**

Furthermore, every day at practice, Jenner challenged himself to never say the words, "could've" or "should've won" and learned how to exorcise the "ifs" from his thought processes by facing and responding to them every day. By omitting "could've" and "would've" and using "if" as a motivational tool, Jenner turned a negative thought process into a positive motivational force which helped him to succeed.

I have found the following four principles that can help inspire motivation:

PRINCIPLE ONE:

Create commitment from above

In too many situations when individuals are asked if they understand what they do, why they are there, and how their job fits into the overall picture, most reply "No. Why?"

Perhaps this occurs because no one ever took the time to communicate to employees what they are supposed to do and why they should follow policies, practices and procedures. As I have mentioned and addressed countless times in the classroom and to conference attendees, training is the "what" and education is the "why."

"If I cannot brag of knowing something, then I brag of not knowing it."
—Ralph Waldo Emerson

Leaders, trainers, coaches, and mentors, in fact, everyone who deals with individuals in the workplace, must communicate both the "what" and the "why" of their particular task. This is necessary because it enhances individual effectiveness, competency, and improves morale.

Apparently, this type of communication does not take place. Often organizational culture just expects that people will learn on the job, and that they will learn from their mistakes.

PRINCIPLE TWO:

Establish trust

Trust is defined in Webster's Collegiate Dictionary as, "Having confidence in the truthfulness of someone or to place trust or confidence in someone or something." It is an intangible principle and trying to define it is like asking someone to define the value of their lungs or kidneys. It is impossible to place a value on them until faced to live without a lung or kidney, then one realizes their importance.

It is simply a matter of keeping your word; meaning what you say and saying what you mean. In other words, telling the truth. When you tell the truth and keep your word, your credibility increases and people begin to increase the trust and respect they have for you.

> **"If I take care of my character, my reputation will take care of itself."**
> **—D. L. Moody**

Having trust for others is a sequential process—you must first experience self-trust before you can trust others. To develop personal integrity and establish the trust of others, you must maintain personal accountability and keep what people tell you in confidence.

Trust extended is trust earned. When individuals believe they are trusted, they are more willing to initiate ideas and volunteer information they may otherwise keep to themselves. Also, when a leader communicates his or her faith in their team, the team members will want to work harder to justify that trust and fulfill the leader's expectations. Noted philosopher Blaise Pascal said, "We know the truth, not only by the reason, but by the heart."

PRINCIPLE THREE:

Provide open communications

Kara Dowers, of Designs On You encourages each of her company's sales representatives to call the president, creative director, or financial advisor with ideas. When they say, "I have an idea," the company responds, "What is it?"

No idea is discarded regardless of how impractical it may first sound, and they do not "shoot the messenger." Open communications cannot be accomplished in a vacuum. You must get out from behind your desk, walk around and visit with your employees and make this a regular part of your daily routine.

I have heard it said, "You cannot, not communicate."

PRINCIPLE FOUR:

Show appreciation

> "He who loves a pure heart and whose speech is gracious will have the king for his friend"
> —Proverbs 22:11 (NIV)

"Any time you make someone feel better, they perform better," Dowers says. "Supervisors may tell others how much they appreciate their staff but often forget to tell the employees directly."

Rewarding an employee is as simple as a pat on the back, saying, "Thank you," or giving recognition in front of peers and customers.

Incentives such as this are becoming more important in a world where, according to a poll by the career web site Monster.com, 33 percent of workers surveyed say their bosses never say "Thank you" or "Well done" and 28 percent say they heard a "Thank you" or "Well done" last month or last year.

Regional directors at Designs On You, as part of the company policy and culture, recognize each small step. An example might be a first sale. During the company's national convention everyone is recognized for some accomplishment, no matter how small it is. She even hands out a Spirit Award, given for exceptional customer service, along with the highest sales award.

Dowers stated, "When individuals become fulfilled through work, it transcends into other parts of their lives and that the financial rewards become secondary." I have always believed that most people do not work just for a paycheck. They want to be challenged to reach their full potential every day. Employees want to work in a non-threatening and positive environment and one that recognizes them and their work performance. That is a win-win philosophy that is hard to beat. Peter Williams, the successful owner of 23 Sonic Drive-In restaurants in Arizona, realizes the importance of motivating his employees. When an employee suggested a summer dress-code that would substitute tee-shirts for dress shirts, Mr. Williams gave the suggestion his whole-hearted approval. Except for those occasions where business attire is required, Williams is often seen wearing a tee-shirt while visiting his restaurants. As a result, employee motivation has improved and can be seen in employees' dealings with each other and the customers.

Generally, in the workplaces of today, corporations are motivating employees by more flexible work schedules, job sharing, and telecommuting. They also want the leader to uphold "psychological contracts" which are the unwritten promises representing good work. This in turn creates a working environment based on the principles of trust and open communication.

No matter what program or process is put into place, employees will not work if the boss is not willing to keep the promises made. Employees, in turn, want to know they can trust their leaders to keep their word and to honestly listen to them.

Some of the biggest motivators are often the little things that do not necessarily have to do with work. These motivators are trust, respect, open communication, a willingness to really listen, and a healthy working environment. These are but a few of the reasons individuals enjoy what they do and where they work.

In addition, some of the most under-used motivators in the English language are three simple words: "Thank you" and "Please." Conversely, the four most common replies people hear too often include, "You did what?" or, "It's your fault," or, "I didn't know," or, "Nobody told me."

Carol Hymowitz, writing in the Orange County (CA) Register, Business Monday Section, June 17, 2002, says that executives can find ways to inspire workers to work harder and to, "Woo new business, plus do the work once handled by larger staffs. Executives can't rely on traditional financial incentives. Instead, they must use creative and inexpensive perks – all handed down using solid leadership skills."

> **"Nature has given to men one tongue, but two ears that we may hear from others twice as much as we speak."**
> **—Epictetus**

For example, Bob Jeffrey, president of the North America division of the J. Walter Thompson Advertising Agency, says he motivates his staff by relying on, "Simple, old-fashioned values, such as recognizing people to make sure they feel connected to the company." The model he has used involves ensuring he knows the challenges employees face in their personal lives. When he learned that one employee was going through a divorce, he helped her out by easing her workload and adjusting her schedule. He also tries to ensure that every employee feels a sense of ownership in the agency. His biggest challenge since coming to J. Walter Thompson after running his own small agency is, "Trusting people to have high standards. The trust breeds commitment." Bob Jeffrey goes further by saying that he wants people who want his job.

Other organizations try to keep their employees informed about the business. Thomas J. Corcoran, Chief Executive Officer at FelCor Lodging Trust, an Irving, Texas hotel real-estate investment trust, has shared with his staff the monthly report he used to give only to company directors. "An employee suggested I do that," he says, "and I thought it was a very good idea – a way to help everyone feel more a part of things." He stated that he always hated bosses who kept their doors closed. "When you do that," he says, "your staff is going to get paranoid and worried about what is going on even when there's no cause." Another novel way he uses to build bonds between him and his staff is once a month he either cooks lunch for his staff or selects a cooking team to prepare a meal in the company's well-equipped kitchen. "It's not a gourmet contest," he says. "It's about serving good food and sitting down together. People work better if they like where they work and feel part of a community."

Carol Kinsey Goman of Kinsey Consulting Services offers leaders the following "do's" and "don'ts" for communicating with employees, especially in tough times.

- DO give people honest, direct and comprehensive information.

- DON'T hold back bad news. You are working with intelligent adults. Treat them that way.

- DO put messages into context so that recipients come away with insights as well as facts. Don't just tell people "what"; tell them "why, how and where their job fits into the larger picture," too.

- DON'T make the communication a one-way street. The more interaction you can build into your communications, the better.

- DO communicate first through action, then words. What you do in the hallways is even more important than what you say in the meeting.

- DON'T forget that one of the most important parts of communication is listening. And you must really listen – giving people your full attention, asking for clarification about things you do not understand and treating people's ideas and concerns as crucial to the organization's success.

Value-Centered Leadership suggests that the highest level of human motivation derives from a sense of personal contribution which is knowing that you are appreciated and recognized. Its core philosophy is that the employees are stewards. They are treated as valuable organizational resources who discover, develop, and manage all other assets. Each person is recognized as a free agent who is capable of tremendous achievement, not as a victim or a pawn by conditions or conditioning.

Thinking Points about Motivation

- What is your purpose?
- Have you made a difference to at least one starfish? This week? This month?
- Are you visible?
- Do you trust? Are you trustworthy?
- If words of praise were their only pay-check, how much would your team be making?
- If your vision, purpose and integrity draped themselves around you, what would your self-talk look like to others?

CHAPTER 5

EXAMPLE OF AN
EFFECTIVE LEADER

"The diamond cannot be polished without friction,
nor man perfected without trials."
—Author Unknown

I have been blessed to know and work for a number of great people who just happened to be outstanding leaders. I believe they were able to encourage people to follow them because they had a strong faith and were consistent. They also never asked anyone to do something they had not done before or would not do themselves. The words they used and the company they kept inspired trust, commitment, faith, and followership. These people would be the first to tell you that any success they achieved was not easy. However, what sustained them during the difficult times were the principles they knew worked and by which they lived their lives.

To illustrate the qualities of faith, leadership, and a commitment to excellence, there are two people, Mr. and Mrs. Orville Merillat of Adrian, Michigan. They best exemplify these and other leadership qualities discussed in earlier chapters.

Mr. and Mrs. Merillat chronicle their spiritual and professional journey in their autobiography titled, *His Guiding Hand*, published by Coral Ridge Ministries in Ft. Lauderdale, Florida.

In the mid 1940's, the Merillats started in their garage what was to become the Merillat Woodworking Company. The company ultimately became Merillat Industries, the world's largest manufacturer of kitchen cabinets. I met Mr. and Mrs. Merillat for the first time in April, 1961, when I was invited to try-out for the semi-pro baseball team they sponsored. The invitation was extended to me by a college classmate, Jack Feller, who had substantial minor league baseball experience; he was a catcher on the team. Jack said they were looking for "more pitching" and invited me to try-out at Riverside Park in Adrian, Michigan.

> **"When you come to a fork in the road, take it."** **—Yogi Berra**

In the early 1960s with my job prospects back home in Pittsburgh, Pennsylvania looking rather bleak, the chance to play baseball over the summer was exciting to me; to have a job gave me added incentive to follow through on Jack's invitation and try-out for the team. Another factor that influenced my decision was the chance to play at a higher level than the legion team back home. I continued to have aspirations of playing baseball professionally after college.

On the pre-arranged time and day I asked a college friend to drive me to Riverside Park for my try-out. It was on that chilly, sunny Sunday afternoon that I first met Mr. Merillat. Prior to that time, I do not recall ever hearing about him, his company, or how he and his wife started their woodworking business in the garage at their home. But that story, and my relationship with the Merillat's, would soon change. Little did I know the impact these people would have on my life.

Although Mr. Merillat never completed high school, he wrote in his autobiography, "I never lacked ideas and I searched relentlessly for simpler and better ways of doing things." He often stated that his "can do" spirit was a gift from God, which helped him as he doodled on a napkin to find ways to enhance the quality and efficiency of their kitchen cabinets.

> **"Every production of genius must be the product of enthusiasm."**
> **—Benjamin Disraeli**

As he doodled, he often asked himself a number of questions, such as, "Wouldn't it be nice if cabinet doors closed by themselves?" He would sketch a self-closing hinge on the napkin and experiment with the pattern. The doodling was a form of innovation which led to ideas that significantly enhanced the company's ability to service its customers. The customers, in turn, received better cabinets at a lower price. Mr. Merillat often stated that, "If a company improved the quality of the product and passed the savings back to the customer, you shouldn't be surprised when your market share increases." He was providing a better product while putting money back into the customers' pockets. He believed that by doing this, his customers would take care of the company through follow-up business and referrals.

Mr. Merillat also believed his employees were the people most responsible for the company's success and always sought ways to improve their lives. This philosophy, which was to make the company the best it could be, was the cornerstone of his vision. He continually sought ways to motivate his employees to increase productivity and quality, while at the same time reduce the cost for the customer. One important way he was able to accomplish this was by developing and introducing what he called the "Trust and Share Program."

> **"The speed of the boss is the speed of the team."** **—Lee Iacocca**

The goal of the "Trust and Share Program" was to share any savings realized from increased production. The formula that Mr. Merillat and his senior staff established paid the employees half the increased savings in the form of a bonus. The company kept the other half to invest in a new physical plant that needed equipment. This part of Mr. Merillat's plan became the profit-sharing program.

As the Merillats put the plan into action, they counted the number of cabinets produced in one work day--which was a half-hour before quitting time one day to the same time the next day. The last half-hour of each day was spent calculating that day's production report.

In calculating the daily production of kitchen cabinets, the employees included only those cabinets that were considered saleable. The cabinets that were rejected were counted only after being repaired and made marketable. If the cabinet could not be repaired, it was scrapped, and that meant employees lost a part of their profits since the employees spent time producing a product that could not be sold. As a result, all employees became inspectors of their work.

> **"If you simply take up the attitude of defending a mistake, there will be no hope of improvement." —Winston Churchill**

To ensure that every employee knew how the Trust and Share program was progressing, the Merillats communicated continually with their workers so they would know the savings each day. The Merillats never asked, nor expected the employees to "buy into" the company, and never asked them to do anything they had not done.

Mr. Merillat believed his employees were responsible for much of the company's success, and they should share the fruits of that success. He did this via the profit sharing plan, using the motto, "Trust and be Trustworthy," as a motivator.

The next step Mr. Merillat took was he eliminated the time clocks at every new plant that was built. He also ensured that employees were paid for 40 hours of work each week, regardless if they were present for all 40 hours. However, employees were advised that abuse of this policy was grounds for dismissal. He knew there would be times when the car would not start, or a child was sick, but those were the exceptions. When an employee was late or absent, he was trusted to provide an honest explanation.

As a result, absenteeism in the plants dropped to half the national average. Mr. Merillat believed that people want to be trusted, and when he gave them the chance to be trusted, they exceeded his expectations. He believed and trusted his workers and they responded in kind. He was fond of saying, "A man is known by the company he keeps, and a company is known by the men it keeps." He also believed that, "If you take care of your employees, you'll keep them longer." He never stopped believing and practicing this philosophy and the growth of the company proved that what he was doing was right.

> **"Those who stand for nothing, fall for anything."   —Alexander Hamilton**

The formula he used can fit any organization with some adjustments regardless of whether it is a private company, nonprofit organization, or government agency. The leadership must simply apply these and other principles which align themselves with their specific organization's programs and policies. Do not let the fact that your organization does not make kitchen cabinets stop you from being as innovative and motivated as Mr. and Mrs. Merillat. That is a cop out! Remember there is no easy way to implement change. I firmly believe that if you want to really improve your personal and professional endeavors, you will do whatever it takes to make that transition.

Later, as the administrative responsibilities began to take more and more of his time, Mr. Merillat knew he had to add more personnel. He began surrounding himself with other quality people, people who believed in his vision of making the best kitchen cabinets in the world.

He also knew that the guiding hand of God was always present in their lives and it was His hand that "Kept me out of the ditches and potholes that I surely would have wandered into on my own." Both husband and wife knew that any success they had achieved could be traced directly to God and His faithfulness to them. Their favorite Bible verse is from the book of Malachi 3:10:

"Bring all the tithes into the storehouse, that there may be food in my house, and test Me now in this, says the Lord of hosts, and see if I will not open for you the windows of heaven and pour out for you such blessing that there will not be room enough to receive it." —(NKJV)

Let me share a personal example of the caring, committed attitude shown to me by Mr. and Mrs. Merillat.

Mr. Merillat gave me a job in his Adrian plant making kitchen cabinets in 1961. Midway through that first summer, he had to lay-off some of his employees due to slow sales. He was quite apologetic. He had to lay-off those individuals who did not have families to support; that included the baseball players, Jack Feller, Ray Larned, and myself.

With no other job prospects available and with several college related bills and living expenses to pay, I did not know what I was going to do. A few days after being layed-off, Mr. Merillat called and asked if I would like to wash his cars. With no hesitation, I accepted his offer. I started at eight o'clock in the morning and finished, after taking a half-hour break for lunch, at four o'clock in the afternoon. When I finished, I was one tired young man. After the inspection of my work, Mr. Merillat handed me a check and thanked me for my efforts. As I unfolded the check, my eyes grew wide and I looked up at him, and then glanced at the check a second time because I did not quite believe what I saw. The check was for $80.00, equal to two week's pay. He gave me money to pay my rent, bills, and I continued to eat bologna sandwiches with potato chips for lunch the next two weeks. I thanked Mr. Merillat for his generosity, shook his hand, and then went to the bank and deposited the check. Fortunately, because sales increased and the inventory decreased, my lay-off lasted only two weeks, and I returned to work on the assembly line.

The second example of Mr. and Mrs. Merillat's kindness to me occurred about the same time one year later during the summer of 1962. Once again, due to sluggish sales, Mr. Merillat had to lay-off several employees a second time. This time, he told me he had contacted the owner of the Adrian Grain Company and arranged for me to work there for two weeks. He told me that all I had to do was show up the next Monday and give them an honest day's work.

The next Monday, and for the next two weeks, I loaded and unloaded 50 and 75 pound bags of grain and feed into and out of box cars. It was hard work and kept me in shape; I was glad to be able to make some money and continue to play baseball. After my two-week employment at the grain company, I again returned to my summer job at Merillat Woodworking and worked there until late that August.

> **"The only reward of virtue is virtue; the only way to have a friend is to be one."**
> **—Ralph Waldo Emerson**

Many months later, I discovered quite accidentally that it was not the grain company that had paid me, but Mr. Merillat. He had arranged with the owner to finance my two-week job at the grain company and had not told anyone else. When I discovered this at that time and for the thirty-five years afterwards, I never said anything to him because I did not want to violate his trust. I think he knew that I knew exactly what he had done for me.

There are literally thousands of other examples of the Merillats practicing "random acts of kindness" for people and organizations around the world.

Read his book, and that will give you a tiny picture of the real wealth of this man and his wife. Oh yes, they were very rich in worldly possessions, but more so in the way they lived their lives. They always gave all the praise for their success to God.

He and his wife are people of their word, have the highest integrity, and live their faith daily. Mr. Merillat had a handshake that would make the strongest man beg for mercy. He was a true leader in every sense of the word. He was a man, along with his wife, whom I admire, respect, and love more than I can describe.

In his book, Mr. Merillat describes one of the greatest privileges of his life. This privilege was to present the commencement address to the May, 1986 graduating class of Huntington College, Huntington, Indiana. As a high school drop-out with no formal education, he wondered why the college had asked him to speak. Moreover, what could he say to the graduates that would make sense? He wanted to share his heart but was a bit confused about what message or theme to present. He had, after all, led what could kindly be called a hard-scrabble life as a young man. He had traveled and been to places that, as a young man, he had only dreamed of visiting.

After considering and discussing his ideas with Mrs. Merillat, he finally settled on a theme which showed God's guiding hand in his life. He encouraged the students to also rely on God's guiding hand in their lives. He closed his remarks with the set of principles which had been the cornerstone of his life. Mr. Merillat told the graduating seniors that he learned these principles in the classroom of life and hoped they would benefit from his experiences. In May, 1986, this is what he told them:

- "People are unreasonable, illogical and self-centered. But let God love them through you anyway.

- If you do your best, people will accuse you of ulterior motives. Do your best anyway.
- If you are successful, you may win false friends and true enemies. Do your best anyway.
- Honesty and frankness make you vulnerable. Be honest and frank anyway.
- The good you do today will be forgotten tomorrow. Do good anyway. It will let you sleep at night.
- People with the biggest dreams can be shot down by those with the smallest minds. Think big anyway.
- What you spend years building may be destroyed overnight. Build anyway.
- Give the world the best you've got and you may get kicked in the teeth. Give the best you've got anyway.
- In short, dare to be different from many people you will run into.
- If you do something worthy of remembrance, it'll be remembered."

Mr. Merillat passed away on January 15, 1999, or as he would say, "He went to be with the Lord." The Merillats' many "random acts of kindness" will be remembered by many, many people. I am eternally grateful that God let me meet them so many years ago.

Achievers like Mr. and Mrs. Orville Merillat focus their energies on the destination, not the bumps in the road. I learned many years ago that self-esteem can't be taught; it must be earned and learned in the classroom of life. Self-esteem comes from four basic sources: Hard work, learning from our failures, being of service to others, and learning from our successes.

I am reminded of the cartoon strip "Shoe" I read in a Sunday edition of The *Arizona Republic.* In it, the character of the "Perfesser," dressed in his usual rumpled tan suit, untied shoes, white socks rolled down to his ankles, and red tie hanging almost to his knees, pays a visit to the "bookstore" located in the trunk of an old tree. The Perfesser tells an unseen librarian that he's looking for a self-help book. The librarian tells the Perfesser, to "Find it yourself." Finally, he finds a book on how to enhance self-esteem and achieve success. He is certain the book will tell him exactly what he needs to know. The Perfesser takes the book back to his office and sitting at his desk, begins to thumb through it. "Yadda, yadda, yadda," he reads, and skips to the last chapter and says, "It's probably in here somewhere." Leafing rapidly through the last chapter he finds the answer and exclaims, "Ah ha, here it is!" The Perfesser begins reading, "The secret to self-esteem and success is hard work." Then with a look of exasperation on his face, he walks away from the huge pile of paper on his roll top desk, and says to himself, "There's always a catch." Yes, the Perfesser is right! There is always a catch.

> **"You may be disappointed if you fail, but you are doomed if you don't try."**
> **—Beverly Sills**

Or to quote Harvey MacKay, "Hard work often leads to success. No work seldom does."

Chapter Thinking Points about Effective Leaders

- Who supports your "emotional bank account"?
- Who has helped you cross the finish line and how did they do it?
- How many "random acts of kindness" do you perform daily?
- Do you focus your energies on the "road" or the "bumps"?
- From whom do you learn?
- What are the four sources of self-esteem?
- Do you know a "Perfesser"?

CHAPTER 6

VALUES AMERICANS
—AND OTHERS—
CAN EMBRACE

"If one good man plants himself upon his convictions, the whole world will come around."
— Ralph Waldo Emerson

Over the past 25 years, I have been privileged to address many different groups around the country and in Canada. Included in these groups are students ranging from the fifth grade to college graduates.

The message I share with all my audiences, regardless of their age, demographics, educational or professional levels is how I value the blessings of those individuals in my life who have set an example for me to follow; they have become my benchmarks. I hope they know who they are, because I have tried to tell them how much I appreciate them and all they have given me. A few of them have passed on to eternal life, but their memory and role in my life remains as significant today as it was when we first met. They were there when I needed them the most!

I have emphasized to my audiences that the virtues of character, integrity, courage, responsibility, and accountability do matter and are the basic cornerstones of the culture on which our country was founded. Taking the right action and doing the right thing is important and setting an example for others to follow must be part of our vision and legacy.

> **"Wisdom and virtue are like the two wheels of a cart."** **—Japanese proverb**

A number of teenagers have approached me after many of my presentations and asked a series of questions; I found them to be quite profound and revealing. Perhaps you have had many of the same types of questions asked of you; but, when they are asked by a teenager or younger person, the question often takes on an extra special meaning and importance. The questions showed me that the kids, and that term is used affectionately, were struggling with the basic principles that adults deal with almost daily. The questions were framed around current events unfolding in our nation's capitol: about scandals, lies, abuse of power, perjury, obstruction of justice, double standards, deception, and broken promises.

Here are examples of the type of questions I was asked by the young adults who represent diverse ethnic, social, and economic backgrounds.

- "If you're not caught cheating or lying, then are you innocent?"
- "When leaders talk or write about character, why then do they seem to apply it to everyone else?"
- "Why doesn't character seem to matter anymore?"
- "Why do people talk about integrity, then apply it to everyone else?"

These are good questions that indicate to me that some of our young people know how to think critically about local and national issues. They understand that our leaders are responsible for developing and enacting legislation at all levels of government.

During my visits to the various schools, I was surprised by the number of young people who appear, on the surface at least, to have a strong sense of personal values. They are prepared to work hard and balance their school, athletic, and career expectations. Many of them also openly share their strong belief in God and also how much they love their families. Many, I think, realize that material wealth is nothing but quicksand and can trap even the strongest person into wanting more of life's bounty. These young people are also willing to take responsibility for their futures. A large number of them are actively involved in their schools and communities, and also give their time and talent to those less fortunate.

As I told many of them with whom I visited, not many of us can realistically change the politics and related events in Washington, D.C. We can make a difference in other ways, such as studying and familiarizing ourselves with the issues, holding elected officials accountable and voting in general and national elections. We do not have to accept a particular point of view as the "gospel truth" just because an elected leader or others state it.

> **"National honor is national property of the highest value."**   **—James Monroe**

In the short term, we can also influence everyone who will succeed us by helping them focus on several key personal values. The following principles can be used by everyone. They are what I attempt to communicate to my audiences.

Anchor your life to a higher ground

Anchor your life not only to the moral high ground, but also a spiritual high ground. To accomplish this, you must clarify spiritual and personal values and determine exactly what is important. Work at becoming the type of leader who leads from the inside out, not the outside in.

To be effective you will need to "peel the onion." What happens when you peel an onion at the kitchen sink? Once the outer layer of skin is removed and the meat of the onion is uncovered, the onion releases its special aroma which causes the eyes to weep. Peeling the onion in our personal lives often has the same effect because it forces us to peel away the façade and get to the meat of what it is we need to change. It is often painful, yet it is required for meaningful change to occur.

In his book, *Ageless Body, Timeless Mind*, Deepak Chopra says, "The past is layered into us in many intricate layers. Your inner world is full of complex relationships, for it contains the past not only as it has occurred, but all the ways in which you would like to revise it." I believe what Chopra means is that in order for individuals to enhance their success they must first learn to peel away the old ways of leading and managing. In addition, we must "peel away the onion" in our personal lives and must empower ourselves to become better people.

> **"When a thing is done, it's done. Don't look back. Look forward to your next objective."**
> **—General George C. Marshall**

Eric Allenbaugh, in his book, *Wake-Up Calls*, states, "A value driven, principle-centered stance will generate a far greater life fulfillment than merely reacting to current circumstances." When you make decisions that are principle-based instead of ideas that are popularity based, this value becomes the benchmark that will lead your life and, in turn becomes a self-fulfilling prophecy.

Earlier, I mentioned a few basic virtues: integrity, courage, accountability, respect, spirituality, and service. These virtues and others of similar importance transcend the test of time. They center on what you can do and how you can lead your life in a more productive and positive way. Virtues can become the quality benchmarks of your personal and professional life.

Conduct your personal life in an exemplary manner

Seek to establish a daily goal to make a positive influence on at least one person. This is as simple as giving an upbeat greeting over the phone, smiling and saying, "Thank you" when someone provides excellent service, or sharing a humorous story or anecdote with friends, family, or strangers.

When we make any kind of contribution to others, no matter how small it may be, we also make that same type of contribution to ourselves. Enthusiasm, happiness and a love of life are contagious.

Living life in an exemplary manner requires a high level of integrity and maturity. Integrity has several definitions, but the definition I like most is in the form of a question: "What do you do when no one else is around?" Do you have one persona for the public and another one at home? Are you different when you are by yourself in the car in traffic, when it's hot and you don't think anyone else can see you? How do you act when no else is around? It is all about exercising personal and professional self-discipline and responsibility in your daily life. It is having a high level of maturity and consideration for other people.

Your intensity about life reveals the content of your character and illustrates the way you choose to live your life. According to Greek poet, Heraclitus, "Our lives are constantly radiating outward, sending messages to people about who we are and how we conduct ourselves." Are your life and actions inconsistent and filled with contradictions? Do they run hot to cold and back again? Are you are both caustic and kind and does your public self match with your private performance? I have heard it said that we should live our lives backwards. In other words, imagine what we want our epitaph to read and then determine a way that would justify what is written about us. This is also called our legacy. If you had only one more year to live, how would you spend that time? It is never too late to create your legacy! Several thousand years ago the Roman leader Marcus Aurelius said, "Man should strive to achieve a balance in life." He is also quoted as having said, "Live your life as if the moment is your last."

One Sunday in December of 1998, The Reverend Canon, David Pettingill, delivering his homily at our church, Christ Church of the Ascension, Paradise Valley, Arizona said, "We must learn to control our desires and keep our emotions in

> "The soul is dyed by the color of its thoughts.
>
> Think only on those things that are in line with your principles and can bear the full light of day.
>
> The content of your character is your choice. Day by day, what you think, what you choose, and what you do, is who you become. Your integrity is your destiny—it is the light that guides your way."
> —Heraclitus

check. To do this requires that we place God at the center of our lives."

Center your life on principles, not popularity

> "He who walks in integrity walks securely. But he who perverts his ways will be found out." —Proverbs 10:9

In his book, *Principle Centered Leadership,* Stephen Covey says, "We must control our own lives and subordinate short-term desires to higher purposes and principles." He suggests this upward spiral is a "continuous process" of personal growth which leads to higher forms of independence and interdependence – a process for achieving a balanced life.

Centering our lives on principles challenges us to use what Stephen Covey refers to as an, "inside-out approach". This requires each of us to objectively assess ourselves first.

This assessment means to begin with our most "inside part of self," honestly critiquing our paradigms of character, values, and motives. Covey further states that keeping promises to ourselves is more important than keeping the promises made to others. It is a "process of renewal."

> "There is only one corner of the universe you can be certain of improving, and that's your own self."
> —Aldous Huxley

If you desire more latitude and freedom in your job, then be a more helpful, trusted, and productive employee. If you want to be respected, then be respectful to those around you. If you want to be loved, then reach out unilaterally and love the people in your life with no hidden agendas or preconceived notions. If public recognition or admiration is what you seek, then focus your energies first on becoming a person of great character with equal amounts of integrity, dignity and humility. You must accept responsibility and accountability for your actions and the choices you make. Without them as an integral part of your personal makeup, everything else you strive to do will be built on quicksand and mean nothing!

The people I remember the most from college presidents, military leaders, educators, and friends are those who use the principles of trust, integrity, courage, honor, and commitment sequentially -- inside out, not outside in.

President Andrew Jackson said it best, "One man with courage makes a majority."

Acknowledge mistakes, apologize and learn from the experience

Thomas Watson, Sr., the founder of IBM said, "To increase your success rate, double your error rate." In other words, do not be afraid to take calculated, objective risks as part of your strategy for success.

You can not let the thought that failing may deter you from making the decisions you know intuitively are right. Success has its own way of increasing self-esteem and dignity and so does not succeeding.

"The Pygmalion Effect" or "The Law of Self-Fulfilling Prophecy," can fill our mind with thoughts of success or failure. We have all heard the computer jargon, "garbage in, garbage out." Our minds are computers, too. When we program our brain with garbage, the output we give is garbage, and we often receive garbage in return. As a result, this process then becomes the "cycle of life." It repeats itself over and over again as we continue our downward spiral to spiritual, personal, and professional bitterness, anger, and mediocrity. However, when we change our paradigms and begin to think and act anew and program our minds with positive self-talk, we increase our chances for success.

"Every day, in every way, I'm getting better and better."   **—Emile Coue**

Many of our friends and family may be willing to forgive and forget to a point, but we must learn to accept the consequences of our choices and actions. Seeking forgiveness is a sequential process in that we must first secure that forgiveness from ourselves before seeking forgiveness from other people. This is when true healing begins.

Admit you made a mistake, learn from it, and then get on with the business of living. Stop majoring in the minors! Start thinking and reinforcing the positives which surround you.

Seek out and surround yourself with people who want you to succeed, not fail. Those are the individuals who really want to assist you on your journey and do not erect real or artificial roadblocks. As Confucius said many years ago, "Man who bows must bow low." Just make sure that when all else seems to have failed, you do not make "bowing low" part of your exit strategy.

Build trusting relationships

When people know you are an individual who keeps their word, they are more likely to trust you. When you can not honor your commitments, make an honest attempt to communicate your reasons to the people to whom you give your word. If you want to be trusted, learn to be trustworthy. Trust builds excellence in you and in others. Trust and integrity are intertwined – you can not have one without the other.

Learn to listen to your values

I refer to that sense of value as a chemistry or energy that seems to flow back and forth between people. Some call it Karma, others may call it "vibes," or when a person has a certain "aura" or "charisma" about them. Whatever it is, learn to tap into this internal energy and let it guide you in identifying and building strong, meaningful, and long-lasting relationships.

According to author and lecturer, Eric Allenbaugh, "Any value is only a theory until it is put into practice; what you do speaks louder than any of your words. Linking what you say with what you do is the essence of building meaningful and long-lasting relationships." Gandhi said it best, "I am my message." He lived what he believed and so gained the admiration and trust of millions of people who followed him.

> **"Talk that does not end in any kind of action is better suppressed altogether."**
> **—Thomas Carlyle**

I have learned that the following three values will help you "walk-the-talk" and build lasting, trusting relationships: (1) Do that which you value in a way that values others; (2) Always honor your agreements, especially when life gets a little tough; and (3) Honor your agreements even when the other person is not around.

Noted writer James Allen said, "Circumstances don't determine a man, they reveal him." What this means is that when you are living and working under adverse circumstances, your real "stuff" has the tendency to emerge. When things are going well for you and life is good, it is easy to support those who support you, to respect those who respect you, and to love those who love you in return. The real test of your values happens when those same people may not love, support, or respect you. What is your attitude and how do you behave under those circumstances?

Writer, Virginia Woolf said, "If you do not tell the truth about yourself, you cannot tell it about others."

Do not put yourself in a position where others even think you are doing something wrong

My military and civilian federal service career spanned twenty-seven years. Throughout that time while attending seminars, training classes and reading policy letters and regulations, I had it drummed into my psyche about "Impropriety and the perception of impropriety." Or stated another way, apply the "smell test." If a specific situation feels incorrect, and you are a reasonable person, then it is probably incorrect, illegal, or both.

For example, I saw senior leadership tap dance out of a situation where lower ranking employees were held accountable. Some of the employees were fired, or at a minimum transferred or reprimanded, while those at the helm were promoted.

Assess the situation in which you are involved, and if it does not feel right in your heart, it probably is not right in your head.

Cherish family and close friends

I know that family can and does play an important role in life; it helps us achieve balance and overall well-being. Try and recall for a moment all the stories you have read and heard about teenagers getting into trouble with drugs, alcohol, and gang violence. The one common thread in the majority of the stories is the absence of a role model, a parent or parents to help guide, love, and discipline the teenager.

I know from personal experience the role and importance my mother, family, and close friends played in my physical and emotional recovery. Knowing they were praying for me and showing me how much they really cared gave me the extra incentive I needed to get over the tough times. Even now, their love and care enables me to appreciate the good times even more.

Family and true friends are more likely to tell us what we need to know versus what we may want to hear. As a result of this objective feedback, they can help us find our mission or purpose in life. Family and friends, like knowledge, skills, and abilities, are our resources. They are only effective when they are tapped into and used effectively and efficiently to help us grow spiritually, personally, and professionally.

Live life to a higher calling

Living your life to a higher calling is grounded in a belief that we are not alone in our walk through life. It is this belief in a higher Spiritual Being that helps sustain us when things are not going so well, and who is there when our lives are in harmony with ourselves, others, and the world around us.

When you are living your life with dignity, honor, and integrity, you are helping other people see precisely the type of attitude and behavior necessary for achieving a life that has value and meaning.

> **"Thy word is a lamp to my feet, and a light to my path."** —Psalm 119:105

Practice Kaizen

"Kaizen" (pronounced ky'-zen,) is the Japanese term for "Continuous Incremental Improvement." It is the relentless pursuit or quest for a better way to do things, for higher quality craftsmanship and customer service. Strive for it as your daily pursuit of excellence. The principles of Kaizen require you to keep stretching yourself a little more each day by outdoing yourself daily. Continuous improvements are small, incremental steps; however, these incremental gains accumulate over time and will eventually add up to and increase your competitive advantage. If everyone keeps looking for ways to improve their jobs and enhance their lives, major innovations are more likely to occur.

> **"Life is either a daring adventure or nothing at all."** —**Helen Keller**

Noted writer and speaker Tom Peters said, "Good quality is a stupid idea. The only thing that counts is your quality getting better at a more rapid rate than your principal competitors. It is real simple, if we are not getting more, better, faster than they are getting more, better, or faster, then we are getting less good or worse." We live in a global economy and given the world's economic, social, and political climate, it is obvious that circumstances change far too quickly. Competition at all levels is tougher and becoming more global all the time. What was considered good today will probably be viewed as "so-so" by tomorrow. Therefore, every one of us must assume more personal responsibility for upgrading and improving our job performance and taking responsibility for personal growth and training. Our productivity, response time, quality, cost control, and customer service should reflect steady, incremental gains.

Granted, this drive towards continuous incremental improvement is no guarantee for job security, raises, or promotions. You can still fall victim to circumstances even during strong financial times when the organization is enjoying success.

If you commit to making Kaizen part of your daily strategy, you will enhance your personal and professional competence; your track record will help sell you. If it becomes necessary, you will find it easier to resume your career in another setting.

By following these time tested values, obstacles will be met and overcome. The most significant obstacles are personal ones and we must learn to face them on a personal level. By applying the techniques that have worked in the field, we can make it easier to get past those hurdles. We can minimize the impact negative feelings when we face the 'hurdle' and 'handle' it in an organized way.

Personal improvement and change are not someone else's responsibility; they are each person's job. It is about taking responsibility for our career, our life, and our actions!

As Oliver Wendell Holmes said, "Man's mind, once stretched by a new idea, never regains its original dimensions."

Chapter Thinking Points about Values

- Do you plant yourself upon your convictions?
- Do you have "quicksand" in your life? Where is it?
- Are you your message?
- Whom do you cherish? Why?
- Do you live your life to a higher calling?

EPILOGUE

As the sole survivor of an airplane crash, I have had the opportunity to reflect on my life, its purpose, my personal and professional aspirations, and my faith. I was incredibly blessed to have survived and that God gave me a second chance to live. I realize now more than ever that every day we have is a loan and our life is a "gift."

Since that rainy, foggy May morning in 1970, I have tried to live my life in a way that honors God – to be His servant by helping others. I would also say thank you to John Davieau, the rancher who found me on fire and threw dirt on me to extinguish the fire. I thank Dr. Wellford W. Inge, Dr. Tom Newsome and the staff at the burn unit, Ft. Sam Houston, San Antonio, Texas, who refused to let me die. I also thank my family and friends who love me in spite of my foibles and who still manage to laugh at my jokes when even I know most of them are not funny.

To all of them, I hope that I have lived a good life. I hope that I have earned their respect and love. I hope I am a good man.

Since the crash and my release from the hospital, my life has been a journey towards continuous improvement. Striving for renewed purpose with goals and objectives is not an easy undertaking. I realize that in order to live a good life, it is not what we expect from life, but what life expects from us. We are continually being challenged to discover and accept new opportunities and to commit to them. When we do this with an open and willing heart, this commitment and positive attitude will help us to learn and to grow personally, professionally, and spiritually.

Along the way, I have discovered one of life's truisms; life and living are not about material wealth, status, or pleasure. A great gift that I have been given is that I know there is a Supreme

Being, and that Supreme Being is a power far greater than any earthly power, and we all have angels.

Over the years, I have been privileged to share my vision, mission, goals, and my Big, Hairy, Audacious, Goals with people around the United States and in Canada. Sharing my life's story about innovation, anticipation, and excellence is a true blessing for me. Excellence is the cornerstone of my life and it involves my faith --knowing that all I am or ever will be is provided by a power far greater than I.

It has been said that at any given time in life our memories reflect who we are and the life we have lived. If this is true, and I think it is, then I am truly a blessed man!

In *2 Timothy Chapter 4, verse 7* states,

> *"I have fought the good fight, I have finished the race, I have kept the faith."*

I hope I have as well.

The following poem captures the spirit and intent of my messages and the principles I have presented in this book. It is titled, "What Can I Do"?

What can I do to make a real difference?
What can I do to know that we're right?
What can I do to help us keep going?
What can I do to help us take flight?
"Give it your all" is one of the answers,
"Hang in and fight" may do some good too.
But what is the best thing we all can take part in?
What is the best thing we all can do?
"Be honest and caring," and "using what God gave us."
"Keep growing and changing," that's what we can do.
"Be open to changes, and help make them happen,"
"Look forward, not backwards" is something else too.
"Be helpful, not hurtful, build up, don't tear down."
"Reach for the stars; keep our feet on the ground."
"Be earnest and trusting, forgive and forget."
"Love people and work. Give more than you get."
Do some of these things, and we'll make a difference.
Do some of these things, and we'll know we're right.
Do some of these things, and we'll change where we're going.
But do all of these things, and watch us take flight.

Don't wait for your Wake-Up Call. A life whose journey is based on faith, commitment, perseverance, integrity and honor will be blessed with gifts far beyond material wealth.

"Ask and you will receive; seek, and you will find; knock, and the door will be opened."   *Matthew 7:7*

Captain George Burk can tell his extraordinary story at your next meeting, training session or convention.

For the past twenty-five years, George Burk has served as a college teacher, public speaker, and trainer.

College-level courses he has taught include: Aviation Safety, Aircraft Accident Investigation, Strategy and Policy, Total Quality Management (TQM), and Leadership.

His training seminars and workshops follow from what he has learned about the value of life and the importance of personal quality.

His story provides a very personal punctuation to his lessons on total quality management (TQM), safety and fire prevention, and the challenge of continuous quality improvement.

He regularly works with organizations throughout the United States and Canada including: Dow Corning Corporation, Sprint, Illinois Home Builders Association, Texas Firemen and

Fire Marshal's Association, The International Airport Rescue and Firefighting Association, New York Firefighter's Burn Center Foundation, British Columbia Fire Chiefs, Adrian College, Ottawa University, CITGO Petroleum, Oshkosh Truck, Pacific Gas & Electric and The Army Corps of Engineers.

Captain Burk also works extensively with schools, has addressed a cancer survivor's association of Humbolt County, California, all of the high schools and three middle schools in Lenawee County, Michigan, including Lenawee Christian High School in Adrian, Michigan.

His articles on safety and TQM appear in such periodicals as *The Texas Firemen Magazine*; *The Texas Fire Educators' Magazine*; *The Quality Magazine*, Australia; *The International Airport Rescue and Firefighting Newsletter*; and the *Hospital Fire Marshal's Newsletter*.

Some of George Burk's Presentations:

Wake up or Snooze—Your Choice. Getting past your stuff. Exploring life's school which teaches us we are our choices, not our conditions. Creating personal vision and mission with BHAG's—Big, Hairy, Audacious Goals. Plan your dream; work your dream; live your dream.

Establish Accountability—Shape or be Shaped. Anchor your life to a higher ground. Unite the inside and the outside. All meaningful change starts from within. The transformation from victim to survivor. Dealing with tough life experiences. Making adversity an ally and a tool to learn and grow. Changing the internal script. Turning lemons into lemonade.

Organizational Self-Management—Moving outside our comfort zones and taking risks. Shoveling while the piles are small. You can't steal second base with your foot on first. The six categories of risk and four types of fear. Managers do things right. Leaders do the right things. The Omega leader. Center life on principle, not popularity.

Transforming Your Life Through Change—A Survivor's Strategy. Applying the continuous quality improvement principles: Adopt the New Philosophy; Create A Constancy of Purpose; Drive Out Fear; Add Benchmarking to Personal Endeavors. Explore the strategic paradigms of challenge, commitment, control, confidence, connected. Turn the mirror inwards.

Passing the Salt, Making a Difference — "For everyone will be salted with fire. Salt is good; but if the salt becomes unsalty, with what will you make it salty again? Have salt in yourselves and be at peace with one another." Mark 9: 49-50. Create commitment by unpacking your bags. Having the courage of our convictions and willingnes to be vulnerable. How much have you learned, loved, and made this a better place?

Bringing out the Best in Yourself — Principles which foster creativity and innovation. Turning challenges into opportunities. To TEACH: Trust, Empower, Appreciate and Recognize, Communicate, and Have respect for everyone. Analyze: S='s A+B or C; S(2) ='s A+B and C.

Develop an Attitude — **A Safety Attitude**. Your attitude equals your altitude. Connecting our personal vision with purpose and goals. Cultivating self-esteem and creating a balanced life. Using faith and a holistic lifestyle to enhance your personal journey. Humor will get you through anything. The presentation includes examples which reinforce the importance of following proper safety procedures, equipment utilization, and materials handling.

What People say about George Burk:

"It was a refreshing experience having George Burk work for us during his summer breaks while in college. He was an ambitious young man, eager to pursue his goals in life. After we received the news of the plane crash and his near death experience, Orville wrote him a letter to encourage him that God has a plan for his life. His life has been a real inspiration through his books and by telling his story to many schools and other groups around the country. George, Orville and I are proud of your accomplishments through all the adversity, pain and challenges you endured. I also want to applaud Olga for her support and encouragement to you through these years."

Mrs. Ruth Merrillat, Adrian, Michigan

"Like you, I believe a person's abilities are far more important than their disabilities. Keep up the good work."

Unites States Senator Bob Dole

"I schedule your presentation last because no one can follow you."

Jimmy Curran, President, New York Fire Fighter's Burn Center Foundation

"During the Christmas break, I had the responsibility of directing a three day retreat for approximately 35 teenagers who attend church where I am the youth minister. We had taken the theme of "Heroes: what it takes to be one." Mr. Burk came to speak at one of the hour-long meetings. He related his personal experience as to the tragic plane crash and the resulting battle of recovery and therapy. The teens listened with great attentiveness, interest and retention. My follow-up discussions with the youth assured me that Mr. Burk had made a very definite contact and impact with the teens. They were tremendously impressed with the qualities Mr. Burk still demonstrates. He is an overcomer....a hero."

Bret Kroh, Associate Pastor,
Open Door Baptist Ministries, Kansas City, KS

"Greetings from Michigan! In our lifetimes, we have the opportunity to reach out and connect with nearly everyone we come in contact with; never knowing when the chance to actually "tune in"...maybe for just a moment...will occur. I would like to take this moment to share with you, your impact on our youngest child, Lissa. With each of our three children (now 22, 20 and 17) I can define ONE moment when our years of parental teachings and guidance, melded with their teenage universe. You, Mr. George Burk, were Lissa's catalyst...you cracked her "adolescent armor" and gave her vision beyond her present experiences. Thank you for your assistance as a motivational speaker, it must be difficult o know where and when you have "connected...it's certainly that way in everyday life. I wanted you to know that in the heart of Melissa Palmer, you have made a genuine impact."

Sandee Larson, Sand Creek, MI

"On behalf of the members of the Fire Chiefs Association of B.C. and their spouses who attended the Harrison Hot Springs conference, I would like to thank you for your keynote address and your workshop. The messages that you brought to our organization were right in keeping with the theme "Dare To Be The Best That You Can Be" and certainly anyone that I have talked to has indicated that your messages were both inspirational and motivational, or to put it more succinctly, a good "kick in the pants" to all of us. If there is anything that myself or any other member of our organization can do to help roll a rock out of your pathway, please don't hesitate to give us a call."

J. S. McGregor, Education Delivery Chairman
Fire Chiefs' Association of British Columbia

"All of the positive traits that we strive to achieve in our personal and professional lives such as persistence, perseverance, compassion, commitment, dedication, integrity, enthusiasm, a positive attitude and appreciation for life, are all rolled into one truly inspiring person, namely George Burk. We were very fortunate to have George as our guest and keynote speaker at a recent awards banquet for two of our outstanding dealers. George also spoke separately to our Aircraft Rescue and Firefighting (ARFF) assembly teams. George left all of us with a renewed sense of purpose and mission. He instilled in all of us the need to **pass the salt**, to make a difference, to strive for improvement. George survived because someone cared; someone took the time and initiative to make a difference. George has a powerful message and is an inspiration to all. Thank you George for being George! Thank you God for giving us George!"

Mike Crowe, Director, Sales, Marketing & Product Development
Airport/Municipal products, Oshkosh truck Corp., Oshkosh, WI

"My name is Peggy Robinson. You spoke at my college (Vatterott) on Thursday and I thought you are a real hero and ray of light in our world today. I just wanted to e-mail you this quote I found because it reminded me of your story.

"Real integrity is doing the right thing, knowing that nobody's going to know whether you did it or not."
—Oprah Winfrey

"Thank you for your time at our school. I am a married mother of two who was very apprehensive about college but after hearing your story it doesn't seem so hard."

Peggy Robinson
Kansas City, MO

"Mr. Burk, The past four years at the United Sates Naval Academy would not have made me into the man I am now without my interactions with people like you. As a member of the Great Class of '09, I depart for blue skies and clear seas off the tropical coasts of Norfolk, VA I have been attached to the USS Normandy, CG60. I have heard rumored, in addition to being assigned schooling that I will become the Strike Warfare Officer on this fine Navy ship. As I detach from the USNA, I would like to update you with a new email address to be found below.

Please pray for fair seas, smart pirates, and no more nuclear tests. May God Bless you all and thank you."

Alan Walker ENS, USN"

"Dear Captain Burk You did such a terrific job today! I can't tell you how much it means that you took the time to share your wisdom and experiences with us. It was a pleasure to see you again."

Catherine Catherine Roberts, M.D. Associate Professor of Radiology Associate Dean, Mayo School of Health Sciences Department of Radiology Mayo Clinic Phoenix, AZ"

"Dear Captain Burk, Thank you for taking the time to share your inspirational story at our annual tri-site convocation. Your story and comments encourage personal persistence and emphasize the importance of instilling hope in patients and not ever losing it ourselves. This is a wonderful message for students who are aspiring to careers in health care. Your story is one I am sure they will remember for some time to come. We sincerely appreciate your touching and memorable contribution to our special day. Our sincere thanks for making this year's convocation a success! Many thanks"

Virginia M. Wright-Peterson Operations Manager, Student Affairs Mayo School of Health Sciences Rochester, MN "

"Captain Burk, It was both an honor and pleasure to meet you at the recent IAFC HazMat Conference. I enjoyed speaking with you at the wine reception and was certainly moved by your talking during the opening session. I serve as the chief training officer of a fire department in central Virginia as well and president of the Virginia association of hazardous materials response Specialists (VAHMRS-www.virginiahazmat.org. In both roles I have an interest in bringing you in to speak to our members. Knowing (hoping) that this economy won't last forever, I would ask if you could provide me with a sense of what a speaking engagement would cost us. Given that information I could plan for next year and hopefully get an early start on your calendar. Again, great to meet you. Your message and experience is both fascinating and inspirational. God bless"

Rick, Rick Edinger Division Chief, Personnel Management & Development Chesterfield Fire & EMS Chesterfield, Virginia"

"Captain Burk, It is I who want to thank you your inspirational message and wisdom. You certainly have a way of taking all of life's daily issues and struggles and putting them in their proper perspective. I did read your book this past weekend (I could not [put] it down once I started...which is really something for me since I'm not a big reader.) I enthusiastically told my parents in Wexford, PA about my meeting you and your book and intend to send them your book so they can read it, too. I am glad that you made it home safely and wish you well during your upcoming surgery. Take care and God Bless."

P J. Robinson, Fire Chief Valero Fire Department

"George What pleasure and an honor to finally meet you at the Golden Gate Breakfast Club. You are truly a great man and I feel blessed to call you friend. By the way, I am glad I bought a second copy of your book. I had it on the counter and my fiancé saw it, picked it up, and she is already almost finished. She is very moved by it, as I knew she would. George, God put you here for a reason and you are fulfilling Hs plan for you. I, along with many people across this land are thankful for that. God Bless you brother."

Ted Battalion Chief Ted Corporandy, (Ret) San Francisco Fire Department Sonora, CA www.firenuggets.com"

"Capt Burk, I just wanted to say thank you for taking the time to come to the Naval Academy and speak at the Officer Development Seminar. The words and advice you shared were powerful and helped me to think about my future as a leader and officer. Again, thank you so much for speaking. It was an honor and privilege to hear you speak."

MID1/C Jason C. Murphy

"Dear Captain Burk, We had our first Quality Assurance meeting since your December 12 visit, and we wanted to pass along some of the terrific feedback about your presentation! Words like courage and inspiration were in the forefront of everyone's thoughts. People could take what you said and feel good, feel inspired. How important it really is to not let the little things bother you. What a help it was to others that you could share your story. And one of the final thoughts: What implications were of everyone's part in exceeding expectations! Thank you again, Captain Burk, for your thought provoking words to all of us! All the best for 2009—and beyond—from Waterford's Quality Assurance Team!"

Barbara Aube, Head, Human Resources City of Waterford, CT

"CAPT Burk, It is us who should thank YOU. Thank you once again for one of the most moving presentations I've listened to in over 28 years in uniform. I look forward to reading you book (starting tonight!) along with anything else you send my way. You have made an impression and have found many friends in the Houston area. God Bless you and the United States!"

Joseph J. Leonard, jr.,LCDR, USCG Chief, Planning & Readiness Sector Houston-Galveston

"Dear Capt. Burk, On behalf of Florida Adaptive Golf, Inc., I would like to sincerely thank you for all your support, efforts and valuable time to make the launch of American Veterans Adaptive Golf such a great success. Your presentation at the James A. Haley Veterans Hospital Friday, November 9, 2007 was truly an honor for all of us. It marked the true beginning of an emotional and memorable weekend for many. As I am sure you have done in the past, you set the tone for everyone in the room that morning that anything and everything is attainable with support and hard work. The result, many injured and disabled veterans who never thought about giving golf a try came out to the golf course the following day due to your inspiring, motivating message. The love and dedication you have for sharing your message to help others believe they can do something today to make a difference tomorrow was apparent from what we experienced and the compliments we received on your behalf. It is truly an honor and pleasure to have you as part of our mission and we look forward to the next opportunity to have your support."

David Windsor, PGA Executive Director Adaptive Golf Foundation of America Sarasota, FL

"Dear George, Thank you very much for speaking to our regimental students again this year! Your remarks are the highlight for each class and serve them well in all future challenges. I regret I was away Saturday night, but have heard your remarks were well received! On behalf of SUNY Maritime College and our Regimental Staff, I extend our sincere thanks and appreciation."

John Craine, president VADM, USN (Ret) State University of New York Maritime College Throgs Neck, New York

"Thanks George, I look forward to receiving your articles and reflecting on them in my quiet time. Just lately I have been part of the behind the scenes crew in the lengthy extrication of two trapped miners in Tasmania and carried with me the "coach them to commit" article which I used to great success. Keep up the good work."

David Cockbain, Australia

"Dear Captain Burk: On behalf of the Savannah District Corps of Engineers, I would like to thank you for the highly motivational speech that you presented during our first ever "Serious about Safety Conference." Your remarks were extremely well received and your participation contributed significantly to the success of the Conference. Thank you for sharing your time and experiences with us. We look forward to other opportunities to welcome you to Savannah and hope you enjoyed your visit as much as we did."

Mark S. Held, Colonel, Commander. US Army Corps of Engineers, GA

"Dear Captain Burk, Providing opportunities for Midshipmen to develop as leaders of character is one of the Naval Academy's most important goals. Our one-day Capstone Seminar for Midshipmen First Class, in which you participated, is part of that important process. Your participation this academic year was instrumental to the continued success of the program. Our Midshipmen First Class were impressed by your enthusiasm and insightful message. The opportunity to listen to your personal experiences and views of the inevitable challenges they will face enables them to more clearly understand their future responsibilities. Your presence also demonstrated our Navy's commitment to the development of our future officers. Thank you for your participation and outstanding support of the Naval Academy, and especially for the donation of your valuable time. We hope to see you again in the future."

Capt. John Pasko." John A. Pasko, Captain, U.S. Navy, Director, Officer Development, United States Naval Academy

"Dear Mr. Burk: I want to thank you for participating in the Philadelphia Fire Department's Thirty-Ninth Annual Fire Safety Education Seminar. Your presentation conducted on June 20 regarding "Lifeforce: Overcoming Obstacles" provided an excellent overview and a wealth of useful information for members of our Seminar audience. The feedback from Seminar attendees was very positive concerning your presentation. I appreciate the time and effort you spent putting together this program for our Seminar. Again, thank you so much for your assistance and support. If there is ever anything the Fire Prevention Division can do to assist you, please don't hesitate to contact me. Sincerely, Joseph Picozzi Deputy Chief Fire Prevention Division George, I really enjoyed meeting you. You really inspired me. Please keep up your emails"

Joseph Picozzi, Deputy Chief, Fire Prevention Division, Philadelphia, Fire Department, Philadelphia, PA

"We used George as our guest speaker at last year's Celebrate Safety banquet. He is a powerful speaker. One thing sticks out in my mind during his speech. After we were done recognizing the contractors for their safety performance, he took the stage. He congratulated them all and said your hard work over the past year has paid off. But, then he said "Now what?" Now that you've achieved this, what are you going to do? He went on to challenge all the leaders of these companies to achieve even higher accomplishments and to never give up, which tied into his speech about how he never gave up. He speech was spiritual, motivational and sprinkled with humor. He received a standing ovation. After the banquet, I had numerous contractor and government folks tell me that his speech was the best Celebrate Safety banquet held so far, and in large part, due to George's powerful speech."

S. Dean Broek Army Corps of Engineers, Alaska District Anchorage, Alaska"

"Captain Burk, I wanted to take a moment and drop you a line and thank you for the tremendous message you shared with us Veterans Day weekend. I can't qualify in words the impact your survival story had on me. I was mesmerized and feel honored and blessed to have been with you. I would also like to thank you for the impact you had on my daughter Marissa. At seventeen she has not experienced that level of suffering or sacrifice and as we chatted on our way home, I could see how she was clearly moved by your fight for life. In closing, please let me reiterate how grateful I am to have met you and how fortunate I am to know that the depth of commitment in a man's heart is that powerful. I hope some day our paths cross again."

Don Accamando, LTC, USAF☐ LTC Don Accamando, USAF. Pennsylvania Air National Guard

"Capt (Ret) Burk, This is Cadet Chip Reed's cousin, Matthew Whitley, sending you an email to thank you again for speaking to the West Point Class of 2012 about overcoming adversity.

Your visit made a tremendous positive impact throughout my class which does not happen often. Your speech and positive outlook on life will stay with me forever. I cannot thank you enough for taking the time out of your schedule to share your life experiences with us...."

CDT Matthew Whitley, United States Military Academy Class of 2012

"George, The pleasure was all mine. Thank you again for sharing your message. You made a tremendous impact. Job well done! God Bless."

Michael E. Turner, PhD, LTC, AR, Assistant Professor of Leader Development, Simon Center for Professional Military Ethic, United States Military Academy.

"Captain Burk, I am looking forward to reading your articles. I enjoyed your seminars at the Homeland Security Conference. I gave my daughter your book I purchased for her and she started it right away. I just want you to know how important it is what you are doing. You were meant to live that day to give others hope, courage, compassion and a joy for life no matter what the circumstances are. You have such a powerful impact on all the lives you have touched. Thank you for not only serving our country in a military capacity but also in your dedication to make this county and the people in it better."

Kim Holtzapple, York County 911, York, PA

"Captain, I wanted to drop you an email with my contact information as we talked about after your inspiring story. I had the pleasure too meet with you at the Dept. of Homeland Security Conference, Harrisburg, PA. I wish I could have gotten the chance to speak with you more than I did and hope to get the chance to hear you speak again in the future. Please don't be a stranger to the Harrisburg area. I look forward to reading your book and learning from your inspirational message. If you are ever in the area again, please let me know. I think everyone can learn from your message and "Never Give Up" there is so much to live for in life. "

Christopher Zeigler, Cumberland County 9-1-1, Shermans Dale, PA

"George, What pleasure and an honor to finally meet you at the Golden Gate Breakfast Club. You are truly a great man and I feel blessed to call you friend. By the way, I am glad I bought a second copy of your book. I had it on the counter and my fiancé saw it, picked it up, and she is already almost finished. She is very moved by it, as I knew she would. George, God put you here for a reason and you are fulfilling Hs plan for you. I, along with many people across this land are thankful for that. God Bless you brother."

Battalion Chief Ted Corporandy, (Ret) San Francisco Fire

"George, Just a note to say thank you and what a pleasure it was to finally meet you!

Thank you for the 'AZ Buddy' and the The Great Presentation –and the coin!

I look forward to seeing you again! God Bless"

Maj. Chad DeBos, USA, Education Officer, Simon Center for the Professional Military Ethic & Officership, West Point, NY

"Sir, Had the wonderful opportunity to hear you speak at the DOD Fire Chief's Conference in Dallas in Aug. I am the Fire Chief at Fort Huachuca AZ and I talked with you for a brief time while you signed a copy of your book, "The Bridge Never Crossed." I am currently on Chapter 15 of the book. Would love to have lunch with you sometime in the future. Maybe a day when my wife has an appointment at Mayo Clinic in Scottsdale. Again I want to say thank you for your service to our country and sharing your story. You are always welcome at Fort Huachuca Fire Dept (U S Army). God Bless In His love."

Kevin Baylor Fort Huachuca, AZ

"Dear Captain Burk, Thank you so much for sharing your inspiring life story and lessons learned with us at our Southwest Region CSI Conference Awards Banquet on April 30, 2010. Your address was the highlight for many of the attendees of the conference and we have received many compliments on it. One person said, "The speaker was inspiring. His unquestioning faith was refreshing. Thank you for bringing him to us." We are grateful and appreciative of your time and effort. We are also very thankful to you for your generous gift of the several copies of your book you gave to some of the attendees...."

Shane David, CSI, CDT, President, Pikes Peak Chapter, Colorado Springs,

"Dear Mr./CPT(Ret) Burk, It was a great pleasure to meet you Friday. My apologies for not spending more time with you. I did have the pleasure to attend your lecture with the sophomore cadets from the class of 2012. You did an outstanding job. You truly had the cadets engaged throughout your lecture, which is not an easy task. Your message was upfront and honest. Thank you for your positive energy and time. God Speed and Blessing."

LTC Glenn A. Waters, Deputy Director for Simon Center for Professional Military Ethic (SCPME), West Point, NY

"CPT Burk, Many thanks for your service and time spent with us on Friday. It was absolutely an honor to meet you and have you speak with the Cadets. We will remain in touch and God Bless!"

Ronald P. Clark, Colonel, Infantry, Director Simon center for the Professional Military Ethic and Officership, West Point, NY

"Wanted to again thank you for the blessing you are to Daryl Robinson for sharing your time and story with us this morning at Shepherd of the Hills Lutheran Church. You are truly a remarkable person whom God is using in a truly remarkable manner. THIS is the reason you live and breathe! It was our honor to hear you today."

Cheryl Adam, Canon City, Colorado

Radio Interview Comments

"Thank you for being on "Holder Overnight." I am moved to hear your story of your plane crash and also your experiences after. It is amazing to hear the optimism that you have. I'm sure there were many a dark day when you were in recovery, but your personality must have played a large part in the eventual outcome. As the saying goes, '"God doesn't give us any more than we can handle."' I guess that statement rings true for you. I'm willing to believe that a lot of people would not have come out of the other side of an experience like this with that perspective. You are an inspiration to all. Continued success in all that you do."

Peter Anthony Holder, CJAD Radio, AM 800, Montreal, Canada

"It is always a pleasure to have a guest that is articulate and knows their subject matter. It made my job as an interviewer much easier. An added benefit is someone who speaks from the heart with conviction and emotion, in a manner that our listening audience can be educated, encouraged and inspired. Thank you sincerely for being on our program and to express my gratitude for making this interview such a delight. God bless you and yours.

Paul D. Anderson,
KJRT/KPDR/KASV Radio, 88.3 FM, Amarillo, TX

"You have been one of my all-time best and favorite guests. I have callers mention you long after the interviews are over. When you're in town, stop in for a visit. You're the best!"

Mike Murphy, KCMO Radio, Kansas City, MO

"Thanks to you, George, your courage remains an inspiration to little fools like me who think our minor disappointments and tribulations are earth shaking and need an attitude check for true heroes like you. I'll be in contact with you once I air the taped interview this week. Thanks again for inspiring me to do a little more for the world!!!

Casey Stevens, WHCU Radio, Buffalo/Syracuse/Ithaca, NY

"George, the story hit home many times. Smelling the flowers, enjoying what everyday has to offer, eating your meals as if they are banquets, and emotionalizing with family and friends and being there for them when needed, tends to build a bond that cannot be broken....You are an example of the feelings that most of us will never experience. The true meaning of life is to live and take in all that is available to one. What a shame it is that our younger generation has abused this with drugs, wrong diets, environmental hazards and material objects that are placed ahead of feelings. Tell your story to as many that will listen as the bottom line is that there is much more to life than just having a good time"

Dr. Gene (Steiner). Host: "Health Advice w/ Dr. Gene."
KKLA Radio, 860 AM, Los Angeles, CA

Contact George Burk:

George Burk
P.O. Box 6392
Scottsdale, AZ 85261-6392
1.800.769.8568
website: http://www.georgeburk.com
E-mail: gburk@georgeburk.com

Books from Science & Humanities Press

HOW TO TRAVEL — A Guidebook for Persons with a Disability – Fred Rosen (1997) ISBN 1-888725-05-2, 5½ X 8¼, 120 pp, $14.95

HOW TO TRAVEL in Canada — A Guidebook for A Visitor with a Disability – Fred Rosen (2000) ISBN 1-888725-26-5, 5½X8¼, 180 pp, $16.95.

 AVOIDING Attendants from HELL: A Practical Guide to Finding, Hiring & Keeping Personal Care Attendants 2nd Edn — June Price, (2002 Paperback (2002)   ISBN 1-888725-60-5, 8¼X6½, 200 pp, $18.95

Paul the Peddler or The Fortunes of a Young Street Merchant — Horatio Alger, jr A Classic reprinted in accessible large type, (1998 MacroPrintBooks™ reprint in 24-point type) ISBN 1-888725-02-8, 8X10, 276 pp, $24.95

24-point Gospel — The Big News for Today – The Gospel according to Matthew, Mark, Luke & John (KJV) in 24-point type is about 1/3 inch high. Now, people with visual disabilities like macular degeneration can still use this important reference. "Giant print" books are usually 18 pt. or less ISBN 1-888725-11-7, 7.5" x 9.25, 776 pp, $29.95

24-point Psalms & Proverbs — The Big News for Today. Psalms and Proverbs From the Old Testament (NKJV) The Classical Old Testament Songs & bits of wisdom in type about 1/3 inch high. Now, even people with severe visual disability such as macular degeneration can enjoy this essential reference. Macro-PrintBooks) ISBN 9781596300668 7.5" x 9.25, 704pp. $28.95

Me and My Shadows — Shadow Puppet Fun for Kids of All Ages — Elizabeth Adams, Revised Edition by Dr. Bud Banis (2000) A thoroughly illustrated guide to the art of shadow puppet entertainment using tools that are always at hand wherever you go. A perfect gift for children and adults. ISBN 1-888725-44-3, 7½X9¼, 74 pp, 12.95.

MamaSquad! (2001) Hilarious novel by Clarence Wall about what happens when a group of women from a retirement home get tangled up in Army Special Forces. ISBN 1-888725-13-3 5½ X8¼, 200 pp, $14.95

Virginia Mayo — The Best Years of My Life (2002) Autobiography of film star Virginia Mayo as told to LC Van Savage. From her early days in Vaudeville and the Muny in St Louis to the dozens of hit motion pictures, with dozens of photographs. ISBN 1-888725-53-2, 7x10, 238 pp, $18.95

The Job — Eric Whitfield (2001) A story of self-discovery in the context of the death of a grandfather.. A book to read and share in times of change and Grieving. ISBN 1-888725-68-0, 5½ X 8¼, 100 pp, $14.95

Plague Legends: from the Miasmas of Hippocrates to the Microbes of Pasteur-Socrates Litsios D.Sc. (2001) Medical progress from early history through the 19th Century in understanding origins and spread of contagious disease. A thorough but readable and enlightening history of medicine. Illustrated, Bibliography, Index ISBN 1-888725-33-8, 6¼X8¼, 250pp, $24.95

The Cut — John Evans (2003). Football, Mystery and Mayhem in a highschool setting by John Evans ISBN: 1-888725-82-6 5½ X 8¼, 100 pp $14.95

Sexually Transmitted Diseases — Symptoms, Diagnosis, Treatment, Prevention-2nd Edition – NIAID Staff, Assembled and Edited by R.J.Banis, PhD, (2006). Illustrated with more than 70 illustrations and photographs of lesions, ISBN 1-888725-58-3, 5½X8½, 298 pp, $18.95

The Stress Myth -Serge Doublet, PhD (2000) A thorough examination of the concept that 'stress' is the source of unexplained afflictions. Debunking mysticism, psychologist Serge Doublet reviews the history of other concepts such as 'demons', 'humors', 'hysteria' and 'neurasthenia' that had been placed in this role in the past, and provides an alternative approach for more success in coping with life's challenges. ISBN 1-888725-36-2, 5½X8¼, 280 pp, $24.95

To Norma Jeane With Love, Jimmie -Jim Dougherty as told to LC Van Savage (2001) ISBN 1-888725-51-6 The sensitive and touching story of Jim Dougherty's teenage bride who later became Marilyn Monroe. Dozens of photographs. "The Marilyn Monroe book of the year!" As seen on TV. 5½X8¼, 200 pp, $16.95

Riverdale Chronicles — Charles F. Rechlin (2003). Life, living and character studies in the setting of the Riverdale Golf Club by Charles F. Rechlin 5½ X 8¼, 100 pp ISBN: 1-888725-84-2 $14.95

Bloodville — Don Bullis (2002) Fictional adaptation of the Budville, NM murders by New Mexico crime historian, Don Bullis. 5½ X 8½, 350 pp ISBN: 1-888725-75-3 $14.95

The Way It Was-- Nostalgic Tales of Hotrods and Romance Chuck Klein (2003) Series of hotrod stories by author of Circa 1957 in collaboration with noted illustrator Bill Lutz BeachHouse Books edition 5½ X 8¼, 200 pp ISBN: 1-888725-86-9 $14.95

50 Things You Didn't Learn in School–But Should Have: Little known facts that still affect our world today (2004) by John Naese, . ISBN 1-888725-49-4, 5½X8¼, 200 pp, illustrated. $16.95

Route 66 books by Michael Lund

Growing Up on Route 66 — Michael Lund (2000) ISBN 1-888725-31-1 Novel evoking fond memories of what it was like to grow up alongside "America's Highway" in 20th Century Missouri. (Trade paperback) 5½ X8¼, 260 pp, $14.95

Route 66 Kids — Michael Lund (2002) ISBN 1-888725-70-2 Sequel to *Growing Up on Route 66*, continuing memories of what it was like to grow up alongside "America's Highway" in 20th Century Missouri. (Trade paperback) 5½ X8¼, 270 pp, $14.95

A Left-hander on Route 66--Michael Lund (2003) ISBN 1-888725-88-5. Twenty years after the fact, left-hander Hugh Noone appeals a wrongful conviction that detoured him from "America's Main Street" and put him in jail. But revealing the details of the past and effecting a resolution of his case mean a dramatic rearrangement of his world, including troubled relationships with three women: Linda Roy, Patty Simpson, and Karen Murphy. (Trade paperback) 5½ X8¼, 270 pp, $14.95

Route 66 Spring-- Michael Lund (2004) ISBN: 1-888725-98-2. The lives of four young Missourians are changed when a bottle comes to the surface of one of the state's many natural springs. Inside is a letter written by a girl a dozen years after the end of the Civil War. Lucy Rivers Johns ' epistle contains a sad story of family failure and a powerful plea for help. This message from the last century crystallizes the individual frustrations of Janet Masters, Freddy Sills, Louis Clark, and Roberta Green, another group of Route 66 kids. Their response to the past charts a bold path into the future, a path inspired by the Mother Road itself. (Trade paperback) 5½ X8¼, 270 pp, $14.95.

Miss Route 66--Michael Lund (2004) ISBN 1-888725-96-6. In the fourth novel of Michael Lund's Route 66 Novel Series, Susan Bell tells the story of her candidacy in Fairfield, Missouri's annual beauty contest. Now married and with teenage children in St. Louis, she recounts her youthful adventure in this small town along "America's Highway." At the same time, she plans a return to Fairfield in order to right injustices she feels were done to some young contestants in the Miss Route 66 Pageant. (Trade paperback) 5½ X8¼, 260 pp, $14.95

Audiobook -- Miss Route 66on 5 CD's ISBN 1-888725-12-5 $24.95

Route 66 to Vietnam Michael Lund (2004) ISBN 1-59630-000-0 This novel takes characters from earlier works in the Route 66 Novel Series farther west than Los Angeles, official destination of the famous highway, Route 66. Mark Landon and Billy Rhodes find the values they grew up on challenged by America's role in Southeast Asia. But elements of their upbringing represented by the Mother Road also sustain them in ways they could never have anticipated. . (Trade paperback) 5½ X8¼, 270 pp, $14.95.

AudioBook on CD – Route 66 to Vietnam ISBN: 1-59630-011-6 Michael Lund's fictional commentary from the viewpoint of a draftee. by Michael Lund unabridged 6 CD's --9 hours running time. $24.95

Route 66 Chapel ISBN 1-59630-012-4 Route 66 Chapel, Michael Lund (2006) (Trade paperback) 5½ X8¼, 260 pp, $14.95. When the forces of progress threaten the foundation of smalltown life – a small church – five senior citizens, a mysterious newcomer, and one young couple band together in an unlikely campaign to save it. The embattled meeting point of old and new is Route 66 Chapel, a building curiously linked to America's "Mother Road."

Route 66 Choir Michael Lund (2010) ISBN 978-1596300583 (Trade paperback) 5½ X8¼, 260 pp, $14.95..In Route 66 Choir Stanley Measure takes early retirement just before September 11, 2001, and his impulsive decisions participate in an unraveling of confidence in the American way of life. His wife Felicia finds that everything she holds dear is in danger of coming apart: her marriage, her church, her business, and even her country. Who or what can orchestrate the recovery of harmony necessary to sustain the spirit of the Mother Road?

Journey to a Closed City with the International Executive Service Corps

Journey to A Closed City describes the adventures of a retired executive volunteering with the senior citizens' equivalent of the Peace Corp as he applies his professional skills in a former Iron Curtain city emerging into the dawn of a new economy.

Before this adventure, Russ Miller spent 20 years traveling to over 100 countries as Sr.Vice President of International Development. Since retiring, he has served as an advisor with the World Bank, United Nations Development Program, and the Vienna-based United Nations Industrial Development Organization, as well as the International Executive Service Corps.

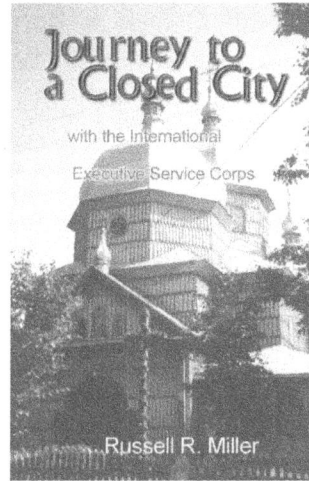

This book is essential reading for anyone approaching retirement who is interested in opportunities to exercise skills to "do good" during expense-paid travel to intriguing locations.

Journey to A Closed City should also appeal to armchair travelers eager to explore far-off corners of the world in our rapidly-evolving global community. Paperback, 5½X8¼, 270pp, $16.95

Books by George Burk

The Bridge Never Crossed — A Survivor's Search for Meaning. Captain George A. Burk (1999) The inspiring story of George Burk, lone survivor of a military plane crash, who overcame extensive burn injuries to earn a presidential award and become a highly successful motivational speaker.   ISBN 1-888725-16-8, 5½X8¼, 170 pp, illustrated. $16.

Value Centered Leadership — **A Survivor's Strategy for Personal and Professional Growth** — George A. Burk (2003) Principles of Leadership & Total Quality Management applied to all aspects of living. ISBN 1-888725-59-1, 6x9, 124 pp, $16.95

Science & Humanities Press

Publishes fine books under the imprints:
- Science & Humanities Press
- BeachHouse Books
- MacroPrint Books
- Heuristic Books
- Early Editions Books

Sciencehumanitiespress.com

Contact George Burk:

George Burk
P.O. Box 6392
Scottsdale, AZ 85261-6392
1.800.769.8568
website: http://www.georgeburk.com
E-mail: gburk@georgeburk.com

www.ingramcontent.com/pod-product-compliance
Lightning Source LLC
Chambersburg PA
CBHW051741090426
42738CB00010B/2370